NAKEl

Papa CJ is a world-renowned stand-up comedian and has won awards as both Asia's and India's Best Stand-up Comedian. He has performed over 2000 shows in twenty-five countries and has had numerous appearances on NBC, BBC, Comedy Central, Showtime, MTV, Paramount, The Comedy Channel, ITV and a host of other international networks. He is the only Indian comedian to have shot his own solo special with Comedy Central Asia. *Forbes* magazine called him 'the global face of Indian stand-up' and *Harvard Business Review* called him one of the most influential comedians around the world. He has taped a Showtime USA stand-up comedy special with Russell Peters and on the American TV show *Last Comic Standing*, he was placed in the top ten from over 3000 contestants from around the world.

Papa CJ has represented India at the Shared History Festival in South Africa and had standing ovations on Broadway in New York. He was the first Indian comedian to be invited to premiere at the prestigious Soho Theatre in London, the Melbourne International Comedy Festival, the Just for Laughs Festival in London, and the Sydney and Perth Comedy festivals in Australia. Papa CJ was instrumental in starting off the English language stand-up comedy industry in India after he returned to the country in 2008.

Papa CJ holds an MBA from the University of Oxford and is often engaged as a motivational speaker. As a corporate coach he has trained over fifty blue chip companies across the globe. He also consults brands on concepts and content strategy. Under his initiative called The Papa CJ Happiness Project, he performs in support of charitable causes across the world.

NAKED

PAPA CJ

MY DEAR SUE

    I WILL ALWAYS CHERISH THE
WARMTH YOU SHOWED ME DURING
MY YEAR AT OXFORD. I HOPE YOU
FIND SOME JOY IN THESE PAGES.

                MUCH LOVE,

                    CJ.

                    SEP 2021

First published by Westland Publications Private Limited in 2019

1st Floor, A Block, East Wing, Plot No. 40, SP Infocity, Dr MGR Salai, Perungudi, Kandanchavadi, Chennai 600096

Westland and the Westland logo are the trademarks of Westland Publications Private Limited, or its affiliates.

Copyright © Chirag Jain, 2019

ISBN: 9789388754866

10 9 8 7 6 5 4 3 2 1

Typeset by SÜRYA, New Delhi

Printed at Thomson Press (India) Ltd.

This book is dedicated to my wonderful parents, who always put my dreams ahead of theirs. Even the naughty ones!

Stand-up comedy is an outward expression of an inward journey

contents

a tight five

In August 1947, India celebrated her independence from the Empire. In March 2005, more than fifty-seven years later, a skinny, bespectacled Indian boy stood up to the British in his own way. As the only Indian comedian in the UK, in front of a predominantly English audience on a stage in South London, he sought to take the stereotypes about his people and his country and turn them upside down. Barely four months into his fledgling comedy career, on a TV show called *The World Stands Up*, he performed the first five minutes of material that his comedy mind had ever written.

'I come from a city in India called Calcutta. About two years back, I was lying in the sun, getting a massage…while my maid cleaned the dishes, the chef cooked, the chauffeur washed the car…when I thought to myself—fuck this life! (laughter) I'm going to the First World! (laughter) It's a shared flat with high council tax (laughter) in an "up and coming" part of Hackney for me. (laughter) For those of you who haven't been to Hackney in London, it truly is a shithole. (laughter) But yeah, frozen food, rush hour on the underground network, terror threats every day…I'm living the dream! (laughter) And given the weather in England, I'm living a wet dream. (laughter and applause)

'But I have been making efforts…to settle down, integrate…be more like a Londoner. I've bought this charity wristband. (laughter) This one's against child labour in factories that manufacture charity wristbands. (laughter)

'The truth is, I came to this country to find a proper job. Only, I've got here and found that all the jobs are going back to India. (laughter) Really, I don't understand what the fuss is about. You don't hear me complaining about the fact that we have no doctors in India. Because they're all here. (laughter) For the same reason, India is quite different to what you might imagine. No newsagents or 7-elevens. (laughter) No cab drivers. (laughter) No bloody chicken tikka masala. (laughter) The whole country is just full… of computer programmers (laughter)…and call centres. (laughter) I mean, I was walking on the road in Delhi last month…and there was this beggar sitting there. So I'm about to give this fellow some money, when suddenly the mobile phone rings. So I'm looking to see where my phone might be…and this fellow whips out a mobile phone. To give him some credit…a homeless guy is not exactly going to have a landline. (laughter) But then he throws off his blanket and there's a laptop computer there…and he talks into this phone…"British Airways customer service…this is Christopher speaking." (laughter) So you see…all this fuss about us coming over here and taking your jobs…what a load of rubbish. We could take your jobs sitting at home! (laughter and applause)

'My grandfather was quite keen for me to come to the UK. He used to say that the sun never sets on the British Empire. Of course, I've got here and found that the sun never bloody rises in the British Empire. (laughter)

'You know, when I got to this country, at immigration, they put me through a "Britishness" test. And I thought to myself, are we so different from Great Britain? You're the only country I know that puts an adjective before their name. (laughter) I mean, why not Amazing Britain? (laughter) Or Fucking Awesome Britain? (laughter) Then even the abbreviation can be FAB. But I mean, are we so different? Half of your public transportation is bollocks. (laughter) Half of our public transportation is bullocks. (laughter) You waste far too much time talking to somebody who you think is an idiot at the other end of a call centre telephone call. So do we! (laughter) You show sex in your movies. We show men and women running around flowers and trees (laughter)…yet we've hit a population of 1.1 billion (laughter and applause) apparently through crosspollination. (laughter)

'So, like I was saying, they put me through this Britishness test. The most confusing multiple choice questions. Complete the sentence:

To be or not to

A: Be (laughter)

B: See (laughter)

'I mean, of course I passed. Then this officer comes up to me and he says, "Your English, your English, is pretty good for an Indian INNIT".

'I said, 'Well, you're not doing too bad yourself. (laughter and applause) For a man with no career prospects and a looming pensions crisis. (laughter) By the way, it's not "innit", it's "isn't it" motherfucker! (laughter)

'You see, you can't afford to mess with us Indians. You may have ruled us for 200 years…but you didn't expect us to follow you back, did you! (laughter and applause)

'If you've been upset by anything I've said today, I don't give a shit. (laughter and applause) Heck, I come from the land of the Kama Sutra, I could fuck you in more ways than you can count!' (laughter and applause)

before we begin

I believe there are a few good reasons why people write books. Rest assured that money isn't one of them, because writers get paid crap. And not the crap of a cat who has eaten coffee beans which are cleaned up after the feline's bowel movement and then sold as the most expensive coffee in the world. It's more like the crap of someone who's been on a fast. For a decade.

Then why do people write? The first reason is that there is a story inside them that they are just dying to tell. That's not my reason because I already tell my stories on stage where the gratification is not only higher but instant as well. The second reason for writing a book is the ego trip. To see their name in print, to maybe have the phrase 'bestselling author' against their name. That is totally why I'm writing this book. So that I can walk past the bookshop at Delhi airport and see my name on the shelves; so that I can slow my pace as I walk past it to make people in the vicinity wonder, 'Oh, isn't that the same guy whose face is on that book?' Yes, I am THAT shallow. It will also allow me to feel just a little bit intellectual and make up for some of the bottom-of-the-barrel sexual innuendo that I occasionally throw around on stage.

So, anyway, if you read the book and like it, please tell all your friends and share a photograph of yours with it on every social media platform possible. And if you hate the book, tell all your enemies that the book is awesome so they can waste their time and money on it. I'd hate to spend my own money buying my own books just to get the title of 'bestselling author'. I will if I have to, but I'd rather give you guys the first shot. 'Coz I'm a gentleman. At least, that's what she said!

BUT I'VE ALREADY SEEN *NAKED*

If you've seen the show, don't worry, this book contains a lot more than what you saw and heard there. The nature of stand-up comedy is that we try and remove every extra word so we can get to the punchline as soon as possible. With a book, however, I have the luxury of giving you the backstory and all the gory, juicy details. Which is a nicer way of saying that I have to pad it up to meet the word count assigned by my publisher. That way, we can fill up the pages and you, dear reader, don't feel like you're paying too much for a really skinny book. After all, this is the publishing industry and not fashion!

NO PRESSURE

The book is so much better than the film—how many times have we all heard that? And here I am, trying to ensure that this book is much better than the show. I'll state upfront that this isn't going to be easy because it is a brilliant show (I hear authors possess narcissism in spades, I'm just trying to play the part). What makes the task even harder is that my memory, particularly the short-term one, is terrible. What makes the task even harder is that my memory, particularly the short-term one, is terrible. If you didn't get the joke and thought that was a misprint, you're going to find this book a very difficult read!

So, what lies ahead of you are fragments of my life cobbled together from fragments of my memory. Luckily for you, I remember mostly the interesting bits. Enjoy!

ground zero

My father was the son of an officer in the Indian civil services. His childhood was spent in different parts of the country since my grandfather's job required him to be transferred every few years. While the moves were frequent, the upside was that the government job came with a certain status and the luxury of large homes. This allowed my father to indulge in his greatest passion: animals. Growing up, he had every kind of pet you could think of: dogs, deer, white mice, and even a baby squirrel that used to live in his pocket. In the districts where my grandfather worked, when the locals discovered that my dad loved animals, they would just drop off whichever animals they happened to find. As a result, for a short time in Lucknow, my father had a leopard cub as a pet.

At the age of ten, while visiting the Maharaja of Sirmur at the Chilla sanctuary (it was a hunting block in those days), he also made friends with a huge tusker elephant. My father, then ten years old, would go alone with the tusker to the river, Mowgli-like, scrub him with stones and give him a bath. He would ride back to his room on the elephant's back, hang from his ear, then step on his knee and jump to the ground. The elephant whisperer that dad had become followed this ritual every morning, all through that one-week trip.

Dad was always an outdoorsman. In 1968, as a trainee at the Himalayan Mountaineering Institute in Darjeeling, he saw a man on a horse riding into the sunset. When he enquired who the rider was, the school principal told him that he was a tea planter. At that moment, my dad decided that he was also going to become one. So, in 1969, at the age of twenty-one, with one suitcase in hand, my dad took a train to the northeastern state of Assam to become a planter and find his own sunset.

My mother, on the other hand, grew up in the bustling city of Bombay, now Mumbai. Her father was a businessman. She was the youngest of seven siblings because there wasn't a television set in their house. And if there was one, either the programming was terribly dull or there were frequent power outages. Kudos to my grandfather for being able to find the time and space to get action in a small house that already had six children in it. Clearly, he was a master of the underappreciated art of stealth sex.

My mother was a rebel from a young age. Since my grandfather was quite strict and she wasn't allowed to go to parties or picnics, she would find ways to get out of the house by enrolling in different courses, including training to be a nursery teacher and an interior designer, learning French, and taking up a beautician's course. She was fiercely inclined towards learning and living life on her own terms. She was not allowed to go out of the building without good reason, so she would sneak out with the excuse that she had to meet a friend on the first floor, then find her way out of the building without being seen by jumping over a wall. Naturally, when she went to Delhi to be introduced to my father, she had no intention of actually marrying him. She had arranged for an interview with Air India in the hope that she would get a job as a member of the cabin crew and travel the world. She hadn't told her family about the interview because they would never have agreed to it. She would pick that fight if she actually landed the job.

So, when my mother went to my father's house for tea, she didn't ask him any questions. In fact, since Indian girls from good families were expected to be demure, she spent most of the time with her head bowed and didn't even look at his face. That night, my paternal grandmother called and asked if my mother could come over the following morning to meet her sister. Mum, not being a morning person, struggled to wake up in the morning, spilled a drink on a white sofa at my future grand-aunt's home and had her saree come loose and almost fall off during the meeting. Again, she hardly saw my father's face and, when he came out of the house with her to see her off, she wondered why he kept standing so close to her. It took her a minute to realise that her heel was digging into his shoe and he was too polite to say anything about it. It was a comedy of errors.

After mum returned to Bombay, two things happened. First, she was offered the job at Air India and second, the day she found out about the job offer, she learnt that my father had said yes to the union. Mum's friends advised her that if she had found a man from a good family, she could always travel later, and that being an airhostess was akin to being a waitress on an aeroplane. Since mum didn't fancy being a waitress, she said yes. Yes, exactly, it was all very romantic! Keep in mind that my mother said yes without knowing what he even looked like. He had already gone back to the tea gardens in Assam by then and the next time she saw him was in February 1976, at their wedding!

Now, if you take a woman from Mumbai and put her in a tea garden in Assam where the closest person lives twenty kilometres away, there's no way she won't go cuckoo. The lack of human interaction meant my mum was bored out of her wits in no time at all. That's when she was advised that if she had a child, she wouldn't be so bored. And so, in March 1977, I was born. I was clearly not a born entertainer because even after my birth, mum still wanted to get out of the jungle. So my father put in a request for a transfer and in February 1980, he moved to his company's head office in Calcutta.

At the Calcutta office, my father tried many different roles, from stores to personnel, until he ended up in the marketing department and eventually became its head. One of his goals was to try and convince as many shops as possible to stock the brand of tea he represented. And one of the strategies he used was to employ an army of housewives. Their job, for two continuous weeks, was to walk from shop to shop all over town, asking the proprietors if they had Goodricke tea. At the end of two weeks, at least five different housewives would have visited a particular shop asking for that specific brand of tea. If the shopkeeper said they didn't stock it and offered an alternative, the lady would turn down the offer and say that she'd come back when they had Goodricke tea in stock. One week after this, the sales team from my dad's office went out into the market asking shopkeepers if they'd like to stock Goodricke tea. I like to think that a little bit of my father's genius was passed down to me.

Dad's innovation crossed international borders as well. Literally. Iran was one of the countries that he sold tea to. At one point, Iran banned the import of tea so their local tea industry would prosper. Before you knew it, the loss in sales to Iran was made up for by selling tea to the tiny country of Azerbaijan, a country with a population of only eleven million people. 'How, CJ?' I hear you ask. Let me tell you. Dad got his agent to bring 400 donkeys across the border from Iran to Azerbaijan. Once there, two tea chests were strapped on to the back of each donkey, one on either side, and the animal was given a whack. It would run straight back to Iran across the border and the payment for the tea would arrive at the agent's office the next day. The elephant whisperer had become the donkey spanker and that's how four million kilograms of tea were smuggled into Iran!

Papa and his papa!

Dad's marketing role was exciting not just for him but for the family as well because it meant that he travelled by plane. For a family that took thirty-six-hour train journeys from northeast India to Mumbai, I still remember how fascinated we were each time he had to take a flight to some place. We would eagerly wait to hear his stories when he returned. Dad would always wear a suit on his air travels and when he returned from an international trip, for the next few days he would convert prices on our regular shopping list and flippantly quote them in US dollars with an air of fake superiority. This was a favour I returned many years later when I came back to India from the UK. 'Oh CJ, you shouldn't have bought me that shirt, it's 1500 rupees,' he'd say. I'd be quick to quip back, 'Relax dad, it's only seventeen British pounds.'

The thing that my dad still can't get his head around is how I can wear shorts, slippers and a t-shirt to travel on an intercontinental flight, that too in business class. Air travel was, after all, a big deal then and it came with its own set of challenges. Dad was once on a flight from Assam to Calcutta which was about to take off. The aircraft reached the end of the runway, stopped, turned around and parked in a secluded part of the airport. The pilot announced, 'Ladies and gentlemen, we would like to request you to deplane the aircraft in an organised fashion. Please do not panic. We have received news that there is a bomb on the flight.' Sorry, please do not panic, there is a bomb on the flight?

Indians being Indians, nobody moved. The Bengalis lit up (you could smoke on planes back then), the Gujaratis started eating the food they had carried with them, the

Punjabis on board demanded alcohol…(I'm ticking off all the stereotypes here). People had to be herded out, literally. On the way out, a Marwari gentleman stopped to ask the pilot, 'If the plane explodes, will we get a refund?' Since it was a national airline, the pilot was in no hurry to respond. He started calling the head office to find out!

Eventually, when the passengers got out, the police were called. The police said, it's not our damn job. The air force was called. They said, not our damn job. The bomb squad was called. They sent two mechanics. These mechanics looked at the plane from outside and said, 'It doesn't look like anyone has tampered with it, you can go.' Then, between two hundred passengers and two pilots, they decided that this was meant to be a two-hour flight, so if the plane was going to blow up, it would blow up in the next two hours. So why not just wait? And that's what they did! Two hundred passengers sat there, looking at the plane, waiting for it to explode. It didn't explode, and off they went!

A bomb threat was not a rare occurrence in those days. In fact, the state of Assam was plagued with insurgency in the 1970s and '80s. Once, in the middle of heightened tensions, when the labourers in the tea gardens needed to be paid and nobody from the head office in Calcutta was willing to travel to Assam, my father volunteered for the task. He delivered two sacks full of cash, 80 lakh in all, and came back home safe.

It was also not uncommon for tea planters to be kidnapped by one insurgent group or the other for a ransom. When this happened at my father's company, dad insisted on putting the ransom money on the company's accounts.

When the income-tax department in Calcutta questioned the never-before-seen accounting entry, his response was simple and clear. He said, 'Ransom money is a cost of doing business for us. Our planters need to know that should something go wrong, we will be there for them. If we can't protect them, why should they work for us?' It was difficult for the inspector to argue with that.

If you want to know what Calcutta was like in the early 1980s, you can go there tomorrow. Time stands still in Calcutta. But it is a beautiful place to call home because the return investment on nostalgia is incredibly high. You can go there twenty years later and find everything exactly as you left it. You'll find the same people sitting on the same bar stools having the same conversations. Yet, I wouldn't exchange growing up in Calcutta for anything in the world.

The beauty of the city lies in the warmth of its people. They are simple people (in some countries 'simple' means stupid, but that's not what I mean!) who have time for you. It's partly because people don't really work a lot in Calcutta but nonetheless, they always have time for you.

In fact, talking about not working, in all the years we spent in Calcutta, the state government was under the administration of the Left Front, led by the Communist Party of India (Marxist). When you added public holidays to the weekends and the various days when people didn't go to work due to some strike or the other, there were maybe two hundred working days left in the calendar. One could almost argue that the red-letter days were the working days. And the culture was such, especially in government offices, that people would get to work by 10 a.m., at which point it would be time for a cup of tea, then at 12.30 p.m., there'd be a lunch break. When they came back from lunch at 2.30 p.m., it would be time for a nap, thanks to the large meal. At 4.30 p.m., it would be time for evening tea and by 5.30 p.m., they would go home. So, if you had to get any work done, you would have to be there between 11 a.m. and noon or between 3 p.m. and 4 p.m. And even then, you'd have to grovel meekly in front of the officer for him to look at your papers because the standard response was '*Kalke aisho*' (Come back tomorrow).

Our favourite public 'holidays' as children were the *bandhs*. A bandh was basically a strike during which no cars were allowed on the roads. On one such day, there was a procession of protesters on the road shouting '*Cholbe na, cholbe na*'. (This is unacceptable, this is unacceptable.) I asked one of the protesters, '*Ki cholbe na?*' (What is unacceptable?) To which he promptly responded, '*Jaani na, jaani na.*' (I don't know, I don't know.) Even in a communist state, a revolution was available for hire!

When I was a child, a bandh was like winning the lottery…only, no other lottery ever gives you the odds that make you a winner five times a year, and everyone wins! The schools were closed and the streets were an open playground for us. We would play cricket and football matches in the middle of the road. More importantly, we would get on our bicycles and ride to distant parts of the town because on a regular day, we were never allowed to go far. You see, the roads in Calcutta in the 1980s were incredibly unsafe. I used to joke in London that in England they drive on the left of the road and in Calcutta, we drive on what is left of the road!

For the longest time, there were no traffic lights in Calcutta. A policeman would control and direct the traffic at the crossings. I use the term 'direct' quite loosely because more often than not, drivers were only inclined to follow directions when left with no other choice. When the first traffic lights were installed at the crossing of Park Street and Chowringhee, they became a tourist attraction. People from all parts of the city came to see them. As more lights got installed, the traffic policemen continued to stand at street crossings and direct drivers to follow what the lights indicated. Obviously, nobody followed instructions. A red light in Calcutta was as exciting as a baseball game in America. If nobody was looking, you would steal a base. You see, nobody really believed in following rules. They were more like guidelines.

Around this time, my friend Tushar Agarwal's father was transferred to Mumbai, where he stole a base at a traffic light, as he had been doing all his life. The policeman shouted at him, 'Idiot! Have you come from Calcutta?' Tushar's five-year-old brother shrieked in excitement, 'Daddy, he knows us!'

Being on the humid streets of Calcutta was dangerous for drivers and pedestrians alike. As a pedestrian, the odds of getting hit by a vehicle were quite high, especially by the mini-buses that drove at particularly high speeds (on Calcutta roads, 50 kmph would be considered lightning swift). If you were the driver and hit a pedestrian with your vehicle, a mob would gather and beat you up. Once, on Lansdowne Road, a mini-bus ran over a man, resulting in his death. The driver jumped out and fled. A mob gathered, stopped the next bus that arrived and set it on fire. It really was the wild wild west.

The only upside of learning to drive in Calcutta was that your reflexes as a driver were honed like a ninja's because you had 360-degree awareness and were always prepared for an idiot to jump in front of your car from any direction. I remember how I laughed while taking a driving lesson in London to get my British driver's licence. The instructor pointed at a man forty yards away at a zebra crossing and said, 'CJ, that's a hazard'. How I would've loved to put him in a car on the streets of Calcutta on a Monday afternoon and ask him to demonstrate the correct way to do a three-point turn. In Calcutta, nothing is a hazard until after you've hit it!

Growing up in Calcutta, we shared a great sense of equality. To put it more accurately, at no point in time did my friends and I feel any sense of inequality. Everyone's father worked for some company or the other. Everyone drove the same car (in those days, there were only two models: the Fiat and the Ambassador). We all wore the same school uniform and carpooled to school. We all suffered the same power outages for eight to ten hours every day. Our family owned a small inverter that allowed us a maximum of two hours of electricity during power cuts. In those two hours, we could switch on either two lights and a fan or two fans and one light.

Nobody really knew whose father did what or who had how much money. One only discovered the name of someone's father's company during the Merchant's Cup. The Merchant's Cup was an event held for different seasonal sports. Companies would form their own sports teams and compete against each other. As kids, we would watch and cheer from the side lines. One of the things I looked forward to was that during the Merchant's Cup, the club would serve fish fingers for free and dad would bring some home.

While disposable income was something my father's job never gave him, it did give him a few perks as an employee and one of these was club memberships. As a child, I grew up between two clubs: the Calcutta Cricket and Football Club or CCFC, as it is referred to, and the Tollygunge Club, popularly known as 'Tolly'. Nowadays, club memberships are much harder to get and the waiting period can be a decade, if not longer. Dad's waiting period was zero years and the 'interview' for his club membership was a slightly more informal affair than the committee interviews conducted these days. He was asked to join the members at the bar at 8 p.m. They plied him with alcohol till 4 a.m. If he was fun to hang out with and hadn't thrown up by the end of the night, he'd be a member the next day. And so, eight hours and fourteen rums later, his membership was confirmed!

CCFC had a boundary wall that adjoined 6 Sunny Park, the apartment block that we lived in. It was a ten-storey building with 180 flats and as a child, there was always enough company. We would often jump over the wall and enter the club's play area for children that provided us with the luxury of two swings. The club eventually put a barbed wire fence above the wall to prevent us from sneaking in. But we jumped over that too.

Outside of the clubs, where the food was quite economical, I remember eating out in only three places in Calcutta in those days. Firstly Nizam's, which served the best chicken kathi rolls in the world. Even now, no trip to the city is complete unless I've been there to have a 'single egg double chicken' roll. My fondest memories include taking the steel plates from our home to Nizam's and being served the rolls, which we would eat in the car while sharing a Thums Up. On the way there, my father would give me mental mathematics challenges and on the way back, he would sing while sticking his hand out of the window and drumming on the roof of the car with his fingers. At Nizam's, while ordering the rolls, he would give detailed instructions on how he would like them to be made and he made it a point to mention that the chicken pieces should not contain any joints. My mum and I would wait for that moment because when he gave that particular instruction, he would touch each of his elbows and say, '*Gaath-vaath ka tukda mat daalna*' (Don't put any part of the joints). As soon as the waiter left, the two of us would burst into laughter. Sometimes he would become a little self-conscious and though he couldn't resist saying the line, he would refrain from touching his elbows. Eventually, he figured out that we were still laughing, only this time at how hard he was struggling to hold back from doing it, so he got back to touching his elbows when he placed the order. I left Calcutta in 1999 and every time I go back, I order in exactly the same way that my father has been doing since 1980.

The other restaurant we used to visit was called Skyroom. It was a continental restaurant on Park Street and my absolute favourite, though we could afford to go there only once in six months. The air-conditioning was turned down so low that I used to carry a blanket with me. My favourite dish there was a dessert called jakota, which was a chocolate dessert that had cream, nuts and cherries inside. What I liked about the jakota was that from the outside it looked plain and simple, but as you dug into it, you found these beautiful hidden treasures. Like the people whose company I enjoy the most these days, those who present a simple exterior but with whom each conversation reveals a deeper and more interesting layer.

The third place where we used to go to eat was Tangra. The government had shut down the tanneries in Calcutta, so all the Chinese families living in that area had opened tiny restaurants as extensions to their houses. This took Calcutta by storm. Tangra is now packed with many large Chinese restaurants and the garlic prawns that they serve are still fantastic.

Our eating habits were fairly normal for a middle-class Indian family. Incidentally, I realised while in the UK that in that country, the term 'middle class' refers to people who are quite well off. I am talking about the middle class in the Indian context, which is closer to working class in the UK. Now, when you grow up in a middle-class family in India, you grow up with a certain set of values. The greatest of these is value for money. For example, I grew up in a house where shampoo never got over. It just magically became thinner over time. I grew up in a house where the bottle that contained tomato ketchup eventually contained tomato soup. Nowadays, people go for holidays to whichever places are on their wish list. When I was a child, if we ever went on a holiday, we went to places where we knew someone we could stay with. I can't remember us ever paying for, or being able to pay for, a hotel room. And if we ever went to a five-star hotel, it was only for sightseeing. Like when the Taj hotel opened in Calcutta, we went to see how grand the lobby was and then came back home.

Similarly, I am amused these days when I see kids buying new clothes for a party. When we bought trousers, we bought them for the next five years. They would be a few inches too wide and a few inches too long. First, we grew into them. Then we grew out of them (the tailor always left lots of room around the waist for the trousers to be opened up). My mother, like many others, cut off the bottom of the trousers and created the coolest piece of clothing that my generation had: Bermuda shorts. That extra cloth cut from the bottom of the trousers was used to dry the dishes. Eventually, it became a dusting cloth. Then it went off to be used for cleaning the car. Then it was used to wipe the floor. Until it finally withered away and disappeared. I've always believed that Indians are the best recyclers on the planet. Because we don't recycle. We reuse. Everything that lives out its original use finds another.

The principle of reuse played a big part in my early life. My mum being the youngest of seven siblings, I have fifteen first cousins on her side of the family. Until the age of sixteen, almost all my clothes were hand-me-downs from a cousin. It's a shame that my cousin was a girl. No, I'm just kidding. My cousin was a boy, but the less I say about his taste, the better. A girl's clothes would probably have been less embarrassing to be seen in.

The beauty of growing up the way we did was that we learnt to actually value things. I used to love the board game Monopoly, but instead of buying an expensive new set, I made one with cardboard and paper. This is a way of thinking that gets into your veins. Over three decades have passed and I can afford to buy a lot more today than I could in those days. But I still can't get myself to splurge on something I consider non-essential. Before I buy anything, I ask myself—'Do I really need that? Have I run out of my existing supply?'

Growing up, even the small things were precious. Like photographs. Unlike in today's digital age, we had film rolls. If you belonged to a rich family, you'd buy a roll of thirty-six negatives and if you belonged to a middle-class family, you'd buy a roll of twenty-four. The camera would keep showing the number of photographs you had taken. As you got closer to finishing the roll, you'd get more selective about what to shoot—the moment had to be truly precious to merit a photograph.

We'd also try and squeeze in as many people as we could into each photograph so we wouldn't have to take an additional one. And even after the dial on the camera got to twenty-four, we would take a chance. Because sometimes we got that one extra photograph and it was like winning the lottery. I can't even imagine what would have happened if I behaved like people do today. If I ever took photographs and they went to get developed and came back and there turned out to be three photographs of my pasta, I'd get a fucking slap!

Of course, nowadays kids take photographs on their mobiles phones. What a luxury! Teenagers can even call their girlfriends directly and whenever they feel like it. At worst, if their girlfriend is from a conservative family and they think she might be in company, they can give her a missed call, she will see the number and call back. We didn't have the luxury of missed calls. We had dial-up telephones, so our thing was what we called a blank call. You would call the girl, someone in her house would pick up the phone, and you would breathe heavily. If she recognised the sound of your breath, you knew you were the one!

But there was always a risk to privacy in those days. Because each household had one telephone number but multiple telephone instruments. If you were on the phone with your girlfriend and your mum picked up the extension, she could listen to your conversation. If that happened, you would immediately stop talking. You'd shout out to her to put down the receiver and wait to hear the click of the receiver being put down. And then you would carry on talking.

But what did we do when we wanted to listen to somebody else's phone calls? We would go to the other room, lift up the receiver from one side, put one finger on the little button below it, lift it up from the other side, and then slowly release the button. Once we had picked it up, we were committed. We couldn't put the phone down until the call was finished, because then the person on the call would hear the click and we'd be caught out.

Those were thrilling times. We would call a girl and let the landline ring once before hanging up. That was the signal for her to call back. We knew she wouldn't call back immediately because then her family would know it was a sign. We would sit quietly next to the phone, waiting for it to ring. You see, we thought our parents were fools. While we were sitting next to that phone, waiting for it to ring, our mothers were in the other room, holding the extension with their finger on that little button!

The one day when house rules were a little relaxed was my birthday. On this day, once a year, we would rent a VCR (video cassette recorder) that played VHS tapes. My friends would come over and for two hours we all got to watch cartoons on the black-and-white television we owned. After the party got over and my friends from school and the building had left, it was the turn of my mother's friends to celebrate. Mom's friend Jolly aunty would come over with a strip of paracetamol tablets. For the next twenty hours, mum and she would watch Hindi films non-stop. They

Admiring my birthday present while my friends watch cartoons

would pop the paracetamol pills if they got a headache but the films wouldn't stop because the VCR was rented for twenty-four hours and it would be a year before they got another opportunity.

One of the first friends I made in the slow-moving city of Calcutta was Zia. She used to live on the fourth floor and I used to live on the seventh floor of our building. After our parents went to sleep, I would write a note and stick it to one of my small toys. Then I would tie the toy to a kite string and lower it down to the fourth floor. If Zia was standing in the balcony, she would grab it there or I'd have to swing the toy so it would hit her bedroom window. She'd then write a note back and tug the string to let me know that I could pull it back up. That was the kind of innocent mischief we indulged in as ten-year-olds. Until the day her father caught a swinging toy in his balcony, broke the toy, cut the string, stuck a dirty chocolate wrapper to it and sent it up.

Zia had a crush on a boy called Chetan. That's a fact she denies till today but I have a letter dated 1987 that proves otherwise. Chetan used to live in the same lane as us, just down the road from our apartment building, in a house with a garden. He and I went on to become best friends and he features in many of my life's adventures.

When Zia's parents moved to Bombay, she was made to join the boarding at her school, La Martiniere for Girls. It's fair to say she was quite miserable there. One Sunday, Chetan and I went to visit her at school. Now, boys were not allowed into the school unless they were close relatives or had some kind of authority letter from the parents. We walked up confidently to the burly guard at the gate and stated that we had come to see Zia Nariman. On being asked who we were, we promptly said we were her brothers who had come all the way from Bombay to see her. Of course, the guard immediately knew that we were lying because nobody sends two fourteen-year-old kids on a thirty-six-hour train journey to see their sixteen-year-old sister for two hours on a Sunday. He said to us, '*Tum itna door se ladki ko dekhne aaya hai?*' (You've come all this way to see a girl?) Realising our ploy hadn't worked, I responded, '*Nahi saale, tere ko dekhne aaya hai!*' (No fucker, we've come to see you!) He chased us down the street with a stick in his hand. Half an hour later, we jumped over the school boundary wall and went to see Zia in her dormitory. Bending the rules (ones that I don't agree with) and issues with authority figures are two traits that have clearly been passed on to me through my mother's genes.

Zia, Chetan and I circa 1993

It wasn't like handling me was easy for my mother, either. I was a naughty child, but because I was also intelligent (I stress on the word 'was'), I got away with it. I would always finish my school work on time or early, and since my teachers were not equipped to cater to children of different abilities, I'd get up to mischief. When I was seven years old, my mother was summoned to school because I had been

My badass and incredibly gorgeous mother

using 'foul' language. Our very strict teacher, Mrs John, wrote to her, asking her to come and see her in class. Of course, my mother didn't appreciate this unturndownable invitation. Their rather brief conversation went something like this:

Mum: Why have you called me to school?

Mrs John: Your son has been using foul language.

Mum: What did he say?

Mrs John: I said I was going to give a test on Monday and he said, 'Oh shit'.

Mum: Oh shit! Did he really say that?

My mother was never summoned to school again.

Mine was a childhood filled with joy. I was surrounded by other children who I played with after school and I was showered with love by parents who had time to spend with me. While a disposable income wasn't something that was available in abundance, at no point did I feel that I was deprived of anything. Everyone I knew led a simple middle-class life and I didn't think anyone in India, or in the world, lived any differently.

humility by rotation

At the age of nine, I was sent to a boarding school in the north Indian state of Himachal Pradesh. The Lawrence School, Sanawar is nestled in the lower Himalayas at a height of about 5000 feet above sea level. This co-ed boarding school has a stunning 140-acre campus covering an entire hilltop. What I didn't know at the time was that I was sent there because my father's job was a little unstable and my parents wanted to ensure that in case they had to move jobs or cities, my schooling would not be disrupted.

First day of school

I made one visit to see the school before I joined. The only thing I remember of it is that the shorts the girls wore to play sports were shorter than any mini-skirts I had seen in my life. I don't know if that was a deciding factor, but it must have meant something if that's the only thing I remember. My body was obviously producing above average amounts of testosterone at the age of nine.

Getting to school involved quite a journey if you lived in Calcutta. From Howrah station we caught a train called the Kalka Mail that took thirty-six hours to get to Kalka station, from where we had a ninety-minute bus ride up to school. In later years, this was changed to the Rajdhani Express, an overnight train to Delhi, after which we got on the Himalayan Queen that got us to Kalka. The Calcutta School Party (School Party was when the school organised your travel to and from your home city, as opposed to Home Party, where your parents picked you up and dropped you to school at the start and end of term) had children not only from Calcutta but also from the northeastern states of India. So we'd have an entire train compartment dedicated to the fifty-seventy children travelling together, along with the unfortunate couple of staff members assigned to manage the lot. Farewells could be emotional at the railway station, but thirty minutes into the train journey multiple conversations would kick off and homesickness would quickly be pushed to the back of our minds. We were too busy trying to find out who'd had the most fun on their holiday and what food (or 'tuck' as we called it) was being carried back to school.

I seem to have it in my mind (possibly having brainwashed myself) that I was never homesick, always loved school, and was very macho and brave. On one of those trips back to school, when my parents dropped me to the station, I asked them to leave before the train departed. When they didn't, I asked them again. I wanted to show the kids around me that I was tough and not the clingy type who would cry and miss his parents. My mother told me that they were going to stay on anyway and chat with the other parents and if I didn't want to hang out with them, I was welcome to go to my berth and spend time with my friends. Of course, her take on this now is that I wanted to cry and didn't want them to see me do so.

As tough as I would like to think I was, I'm one hundred per cent sure that my mother's version is the truth. Till date, if I'm troubled by something, I tend to not share it with my parents. Not because I'm not close to them or am uncomfortable sharing things, but because I don't want to have them stress about it. I'd rather have a crack at fixing it myself first. It's only when options within the range of my own capabilities have been exhausted that I reach out for help. This is a trait I've definitely picked up from my father. In all these years, I'm yet to hear him complain about anything. He might casually mention that he has high temperature, that it's probably a viral, and that it will go away in due course. He then thumps his chest and goes back into his cave!

For a boy who hadn't left home until the age of nine, I settled into boarding school quite well. With boarding schools, you either fit in or you don't. There's rarely a middle ground. Luckily for me, I fit.

Classes in the junior school, or prep school as it was called, took place from Monday to Saturday. The last class on Saturday was 'letter writing class'. In the early days, I was reasonably diligent about writing and my father still has a file that contains all the letters I wrote to them from school. I'd like to say my early diligence was because I wanted to ensure that communication between my parents and their only child was regular, transparent and filled with love so that the wonderful connection I had with them would remain eternally beautiful. However, the fact was that our teachers gave us our weekly pocket money only after we submitted our letters and so it had to be done! By the time I got to senior school, where there was no letter writing class, my parents would just give me stamped and pre-addressed envelopes and tell me to post one every week so they knew I was alive.

When I joined Sanawar in 1986, we didn't have mobile phones. Email had not yet been invented and telephone calls were very rarely made and that, too, only in case of an emergency. Letter writing was really the only form of communication and oh, what joy it was to receive a handwritten letter. There was an entire ceremony that took place before the letter was read. You'd first try and guess who it was from by looking at the handwriting on the envelope. Then you'd hold the envelope against the light to ensure no part of the letter was torn when you opened it. Your heart would beat with even more excitement when the envelope had the words 'DO NOT BEND. PHOTOGRAPHS ENCLOSED' written on it in capital letters. That, of course, presented a delicious dilemma when you opened it—should you read the letter first or look at the photograph? And even when you had the photograph in your hand, should you look at the image first or at what was written behind it? The entire process was like when you eat a meal—some people eat their favourite dish first and some people save it for the end so that the taste remains in your mouth. (It's like some people's approach to sex. There are some positions that are your favourites. You may start with something specific and jumble it up in the middle, but more often than not, you know what you want to end on!)

When I joined school, our pocket money was two rupees a week. It was increased to five, then fifteen, then twenty-five. By the time I left school nine years later, I was entitled to the princely sum of two hundred and fifty rupees a month. The maximum pocket money I ever got from home during prep school was sixty-five rupees for a four-month term. The school had a tuck shop where one could buy tuck on a Sunday. The food we got from home never lasted long because if you didn't share it with the others soon enough, they would break into your trunk or your locker (a little wooden cupboard that held all your belongings) and steal it.

A 'system' we had in place at boarding-school was of 'sharing partners'. You and one other person (it could be more, but was normally one) decided that you would share the food that each of you brought to school from home. You were obliged to share half of what you had with your partner. The term of this contract was one school term, during which, like canvassing talent for a sports league, you looked around to see what kind of tuck others had got, so you could find a more lucrative sharing partner the following term.

Of the tuck we could buy in school, my favourite item was a little orange sweet. We got ten for one rupee. A packet of glucose biscuits also cost one rupee. Sometimes a bunch of us pooled in and bought a tin of condensed milk, into which we would dip our glucose biscuits. Or we'd just eat it plain. Milk powder was something else we ate plain. Just dry milk powder, poured into palms that we would lick clean. In the later years we could afford chocolates and packets of crisps. We were lucky in that, in our time, unlike today, packets of chips were not subject to the Wonderbra school of marketing and actually contained more chips than air! Of course, Maggi noodles were the most popular form of tuck even then. If we had the luxury of an immersion rod, it would be 'cooked' in a plastic mug. If not, it would be soaked in cold water. More often than not, it was just crushed and eaten uncooked.

Since food was a rare commodity and we were starving literally all the time, not only would we eat absolutely anything, we also invented rules that allowed us to do so. The most famous was 'the forty-second rule'. According to this, if any edible item fell on the ground, 'science' reliably said that it would be forty seconds before it became unfit for human consumption. As long as you picked it up within that time, you could put it in your mouth!

There were times when someone else was eating say, a chocolate, and you asked them for a piece. They would pretend not to hear and put the whole thing in their mouth. Then they would take it out and say, 'Sorry brother, I already put it in my mouth'. More than once I've said, 'No problem, brother' and broken off a piece of saliva-soaked chocolate and put it in my mouth. Desperate circumstances call for desperate measures.

Then, of course, there were the assholes who really did not want to share their food. If it was too big for them to down at one go, they would spit all over it. The appropriate response, if they were not bigger built than you were, was to pull the said food item in your direction and sprinkle it with your own share of saliva.

In prep school, bedtime was 8 p.m., but on Saturday nights 'lights out' was at 9 p.m. On Saturdays we were also allowed to dance with the girls in the common room. I remember that the floor of the common room was tiled and as ten- and eleven-year-olds we would count how many tiles close we could get to the girls we were dancing with.

There was a boy in my class by the name of Advait. He liked a girl called Gaurika, but rumour was that she had a preference for me. Advait was a giant in those days—56 kg at the age of ten. I was skinny and scrawny. One Saturday night, he grabbed me by the collar and dragged me to the staircase below the girls' dormitory, which was just above the common room. He then put his foot just past the tile below the staircase that boys were not supposed to cross, which was a very bold step at the time. With me still held by the collar, he shouted up towards the girls' dormitory in the most booming voice a ten-year-old could possess, 'Gaurika Gupta! Who do you want to dance with, him or me?' This was followed by the whispering of four or five girls at the top of the staircase after which a squeaky voice answered, 'She wants to dance with him'. Advait's face was hit by a wrecking ball of shock and he instantly burst into tears and ran back to the dormitory. I was not as pleased about the young lady's preference as I was about the fact that Goliath had chosen not to crush David that night.

Class seven marked the beginning of senior school and the transition was tough. A combination of fear and hope. The hope that you'd get a nice prefect in your dorms and the fear that you might get bullied a lot. Stories of bullying had already found their way to us from the boys who had gone to senior school the previous year.

In senior school, there were junior dorms and senior dorms. While classes seven and eight were in the junior dorms, class nine students were split up between the senior and junior dorms. Again, you hoped that you were the senior-most in the junior dorms as opposed to the junior-most in the senior dorms. This was good preparation for the circle of life where you'd eventually become the junior-most in college, then the senior-most in college, and then the junior-most at your workplace. A good system to keep your ego in check: The moment you begin to think you are somebody, life slaps you down and makes you a nobody. Humility by rotation.

Humility aside, there are many things that boarding schools teach you. They have their own unwritten laws and these are laws that you learn very, very quickly. The first and most important law is that you never tattle on a fellow student to the faculty. It is the easiest way to ensure that you instantly become a social outcast. The second thing you learn is that you can do anything you want, but if you get caught, you have to face the consequences. So you either tow the line, learn how to not get caught, or learn how to bear the consequences. And the consequences in those days were far more severe than you can imagine nowadays.

The 'official' punishment imposed by the school was called drill. Drill took many forms. You either had to do various running exercises—for example, you had to run down five hundred steps and run back up the same five hundred steps within five minutes. If you could not, you would have to do it again. Another exercise we had to do was 'murga'. Murga meant holding your ears by taking your hands up from under your knees while keeping your ass as high in the air as possible. Then there was the legs-up-hands-down execise, where your feet were placed on a four-foot-high platform, your hands were on the ground as far away from your feet as possible, and once again, your ass had to be as high as possible. There was also the handstand, where you had to stand on your hands while resting your feet against the wall. All these exercises had to be done for ten minutes and sometimes longer. If you somehow got a medical certificate saying you were unable to do physical exercises, you would get a punishment far worse. You'd have to write one sentence a thousand times over by the next morning: 'I (name) promise that I will never ever go for assembly without my assembly book again'.

These were just the official punishments. Our seniors and prefects usually did not want to waste their time administering such long drawn out drills and suffering the grovelling of struggling juniors. So they came up with swifter forms of punishment and the more psychotic seniors were quite innovative with the torture they chose to dole out. Common forms of punishment included a specified number of slaps across your face, getting whacked with squash rackets on your arse, or worse, getting hit with either a cricket bat or a field hockey stick on your arse. Some of us got whacked so hard with hockey sticks, we were left with Nike swoosh marks on our backsides and could barely sit for a whole week.

Some of the seniors would place their hands in front of our faces, at a distance of one foot, two feet and three feet away, and ask us from what distance we would like to be slapped. If you asked for one foot he would say, 'Trying to sneak out, bastard'. If you asked for three feet he'd say, 'Trying to be cocky, bastard'. If you asked for the middle option, he'd say, 'Trying to be clever, bastard'. It didn't really matter what you said, he'd still swing at you from the maximum distance possible.

There was one senior who would pair us up and make us give each other five slaps each. If he thought the slap wasn't hard enough, it wouldn't count, and he would slap you instead. Given that particular senior was a national-level boxer, we made sure we whacked the shit out of our partners. Also, you had to choose your partner carefully. The skinny guys were often the worst to be partnered with because they would give what we called 'skeleton slaps', i.e., tight slaps with their bony hands.

Then, of course, during the official punishments like murga or legs-up-hands-down, if our arses came down too low, some prefects would whack our backsides with hockey sticks or just kick us. One of the most sadistic guys I knew was actually the head boy of the school in one particular year. He would make us do legs-up-hands-down, but instead of our hands, our elbows would have to be on the rough ground. And we would have to jog in place with our elbows bleeding. One thousand steps. If we stopped or our arses came down a little, he would whip us across our backs with a leather belt. I'm grateful that this form of abuse has been clamped down upon and very surprised at how many of us turned out reasonably okay in spite of being subjected to it. Strangely though, in those days, we didn't see it as abuse. It was understood that that's how things were. Don't fuck up. If you fuck up, don't get caught. And if you get caught, learn how to take a hammering. We never felt victimised or singled out because that's how it was for everyone.

That being said, fucking up and getting caught wasn't the only path to getting hammered. Sometimes a senior would call you and say, 'I don't like your face', and slap you and send you off. That taught me a life lesson that I would go on to forget and be reminded of many times in life. The deeply philosophical understanding was this: Some people are just fucking assholes.

During my time in Sanawar, the boys from the eleventh and twelfth classes were in separate dormitories, one above the other. Except the prefects, who stayed in the dormitories of the respective houses that they were prefects of. On a Sunday, the last place where you wanted to be spotted as a junior was on the quad outside the class eleven and twelve dorms. Because a senior was bound to call you to do a 'favour' for him and once you were done servicing his needs, another senior would spot you, and basically your entire day was gone doing favours for seniors. They were called 'favours', but in no way did any of those activities ever leave the senior feeling obligated to you!

Also, in no way was the favour optional, whether it was polishing shoes, getting water or fetching something from the tuck shop. Sometimes, if the senior was someone you particularly hated, before you served them the water, you'd carefully stir it with your penis. Eventually some seniors wised up to this practice and began asking the juniors to sip the water first, like ancient kings who had tasters to ensure they weren't being poisoned. So eventually we downgraded our invisible protest by spitting in the water and stirring that in instead.

Sunday afternoon brought one of two official activities, or one of two unofficial activities. The first official activity was going for a movie that was screened via old projectors in the big school auditorium called Barne Hall. Barne Hall was built the typical British way—lots of aging wood, wall-mounted photographs of the school bigwigs, a bust of the founder, the flags presented by the Queen on the side, the emblems and house colours. It was all quite majestic, and the official venue for morning assemblies, speaker sessions, debates, shows and the like. Inside Barne Hall were two boards. One board had on it the names of the head boys from all the past years. Another had on it the names of the winners of the President's Medal. This award, given to the best all-rounder, was later renamed the Chief of Army Staff's Medal. Ever since I saw that board at the age of nine, it became my life's ambition to have my name on it.

The second official Sunday activity was playing a game of some sort or hanging out with friends near the tuck shop, trying in both situations to be very careful not to be spotted by particularly mean seniors.

The unofficial Sunday activity involved seniors who were making out with their girlfriends ('making out' is a broad term that covers various degrees of intimacy from kissing to full-blown sex). Since most of the school would go for the film at Barne Hall, this was an opportune time for senior couples to explore not just the hidden corners of the beautiful 140-acre campus but also the hidden corners of each other's bodies, ably led on by their raging hormones.

As juniors, we ended up doing one of two things. Either the seniors had us 'keeping guard'—which basically meant being on the lookout for any approaching teachers. Or we scooted off to spy on those who were making out (we didn't have mobile phones, the internet or much access to pornography in those days, but more on that later). Behind the art department was one of the all-time favourite spots: If you hadn't made out there, you hadn't lived.

When I was in class eight and all of thirteen years old, we heard that a senior was making out with a particularly attractive girl at the English department. Now, the English department was on the first floor and the main staircase to it was locked on Sundays. So fourteen horny thirteen-year-olds climbed up a tiny spiral staircase and positioned themselves below the window of Room Number 3. Sure enough, our man was in position with his partner, breathing heavily.

I don't know if you've ever seen a bunch of thirteen-year-olds watching a couple of seventeen-year-olds making out, but I can tell you this: they are incapable of being quiet. And, sure enough, our restlessness was enough to alert the couple and the senior in question got up. He was a big, strong, short-distance runner and we were terrified. We quickly ran down the spiral staircase but before we could get away, he got to us by jumping from one rooftop to another, and apprehended us at the bottom of the staircase, where he stood us all in one line. This is how the questioning went:

Senior: What are you guys doing here?

One of us: Bro, Khanna sent us.

Khanna was a senior in our house who we were friendly with. We hoped this would save us from getting a hammering.

Senior: Why did he send you?

One of us: He sent us to take snaps.

Sneaking around and taking photographs of people making out was not an uncommon practice, especially on the instructions of seniors.

Senior: Where is the camera?

One of us: Bro, we forgot to bring it.

All fourteen of us got the shit slapped out of us that afternoon.

Three years later, in December 1993, I was sixteen years old when I was caught making out by a teacher on a Sunday afternoon below the science department stairs. She didn't see us. She heard us.

I still remember jumping out of my skin (given that's what I was wearing at the time) when her shrill voice went, 'Who's there?' One minute later, though it felt like an hour, I walked out. She immediately asked, 'Who else?' This was the cue for my girlfriend at the time to sheepishly do her walk of shame. Mrs Solomon, the Dean of Studies and third most senior member of faculty, warned me that there were things in store for me, which activities like this might jeopardise. I apologised. One week later, my name was announced as head boy of the school for the year 1994–95.

Speaking in Barne Hall as head boy

At the Lawrence School, Sanawar, or S'na as it was referred to, there were four houses: Himalaya, Nilgiri, Siwalik and Vindhya. I was in Siwalik house. For the duration of my stint at Sanawar, it was normally Himalaya and Siwalik that competed for first place in sports and most other activities while Nilgiri and Vindhya slugged it out for third place. But there were some things that these two houses were particularly good at: Nilgiri were good at swimming and Vindhya at athletics and cross country. The Nilgarians were called 'commies' because of their over enthusiastic approach to mundane things like winning PT competitions. Their prefects would make them wake up at 5 a.m. so they could do their physical training in sync. In senior school, the Nilgiri House dormitory was quite far from the other three houses, so they were often in their own world and somewhat separate from the others. This sometimes resulted in them being picked on a bit more by students from the other houses.

One day at assembly, Gulbagh Singh, my house captain, a national-level boxer and the strongest guy in school, got pissed off with the Nilgarians in my batch for some reason. He announced to them, 'You fucking commies, you come and see me tonight.' When Gulbagh Singh told you to come and see him tonight, you knew you were dead. He was our version of a WWE wrestler. The entire batch of Nilgarians were shitting themselves. Unable to eat or even entertain any thought besides the fact that they'd get the thrashing of a lifetime, they came up with a plan. They got together and caught hold of a boy from the batch called Aakash Nijhawan. He had joined school recently, and they scared the living daylights out of him. They said, 'Nijjhu bro, Gulbagh has told us to come and see him tonight. You know what that means, right? It means we are going to get a bad hammering. We guys will still be able to take it. What will happen to you? You will die.'

Fully convinced that they were right and that his death was imminent, Nijhawan sought advice on what to do. The batch convinced him that he should run away from school. Gulbagh would find out that Nijjhu had run away, and scared that the teachers would find out why, he would refrain from beating anyone up and they would all be saved. Nijhawan was convinced that this was a great plan. But where could he go? His grandmother lived in Chandigarh, which was ninety minutes away by bus from a town called Dharampur that was an 8 km walk from school. That's where he would go.

A bus ticket from Dharampur to Chandigarh cost thirty-two rupees and Nijhawan needed money. The batch slowly chipped in with one rupee here, two rupees there, until thirty-two rupees were accumulated. It then struck them that since Nijhawan was going to Chandigarh, he might as well get them some food. Hot Millions was a restaurant famous for its burgers and pizzas and they suggested Nijhawan go straight there to get everyone some grub. Suddenly fifty- and hundred-rupee notes started flying about till Nijhu had enough money to feed a small army. They then escorted him to 'Stinkies', a hill behind the central dining hall, where the trash was thrown, and waved goodbye as he ran away from school.

On his departure, news of Nijhawan's escape was strategically delivered to Gulbagh Singh via the grapevine. In the meantime, Nijhawan found his way to Chandigarh, reached Hot Millions restaurant, bought all the burgers and pizzas he could, and then got to his grandmother's house. Upon arrival, he was swiftly informed by his grandmother that his visit was unacceptable and he was promptly sent back to school. He came back in the late afternoon with all the food he had bought, and it was downed at once, with great gusto. That night, when the batch went to see Gulbagh Singh, Nijhawan was the only guy who got a hammering!

Another Nilgiri House tale involved a teacher by the name of Mr Sibbal. Mr Sibbal taught us English. He was quite a spaced out sort of chap; we used to call him 'Zap'. One day, Zap took his wife to Chandigarh for a dental appointment. While he was away, four boys from Nilgiri House broke into his house. They stole a CD, raided his fridge, and took all the food they could find. Zap came back to find his house burgled and, as you might expect, was deeply upset.

It turned out that Zap wasn't as spaced out as we had thought he was. The following day, he set an essay-writing competition for the school. The title of the essay was, 'The mystery of the robbery at Mr Sibbal's house'. The four boys who broke into his house wrote exactly the same story! They changed the names but described in great detail how the culprits got in through the ventilator, raided the fridge, then went to raid the cabinet and left with two packets of Maggi noodles, four packets of chips and a Bryan Adams CD. Of course, they were all caught and got the thrashing of a lifetime.

Twenty years later, I was telling this story on stage at the Chandigarh Golf Club and one of the boys happened to be there. I asked him why he had written the truth in his essay. His response: 'Brother, I thought I'd get full marks!'

Another memorable aspect of school was the unique ways in which the sense of pride in being Indian manifested itself. I remember a sweet boy who went to the UK on an exchange programme. He returned four months later with a very strong British accent. On the very first day of the second term, 1 August 1994, at 10 p.m., he was made to stand on top of a locker and read a history text book. The whole dormitory watched as Winston Churchill himself began to read. Every ten minutes, he received one slap. Six hours and thirty-six slaps later, the accent was gone and the boy from the Haryana village was back. By then, he had almost forgotten how to speak English.

I went on an exchange programme too, to Appleby College in Canada, in the first school term of 1993. The college was located in a town called Oakville, which was about forty-five minutes west of Toronto. Oakville was the kind of town Donald Trump must have wet dreams about—it was whiter than white.

The sports on offer during spring term at Appleby were rugby, softball and badminton. I had never played rugby and given I had the frame of a toothpick, it was never going to be for me. Softball I didn't consider macho enough, since the ball was thrown underarm. Coming from a cricket-playing nation, I thought anyone who needed a big glove to field was a bit of a wimp. So I gravitated towards badminton and ended up captaining the school under-sixteen team. That was lovely because it allowed me to travel to many other towns to play interschool matches.

On 1 August 1993, I returned to Sanawar to start class eleven. Now, class eleven is when you choose your stream, i.e., science, commerce or arts. I had missed the first four months when you could experiment and try out different subjects. In those days, it was fashionable to 'keep your options open', and so I chose science—physics, chemistry, mathematics, computer science and English core. According to the keeping-your-options-open theory, if you took science, you could always move to commerce later, but if you took commerce, you couldn't pursue science. The arts and humanities were, of course, bottom of the pile because, if you chose them, you couldn't do anything later. Which is a lot like pursuing a career in stand-up comedy. The world thinks you're a lovely guy, but with zero transferable skills!

I got eighty per cent at the end of the first two months and ninety-six per cent over the next two months. But I hated it. I wanted to switch to commerce. I requested the change and promised the Dean of Studies that I would catch up. She said if each of the teachers whose classes I wanted to join agreed, I could change streams. Every teacher agreed, with the exception of Mrs Sharma, the economics teacher. She was housemistress of Himalaya House and I was dating a girl, one year my senior, from her house. She didn't approve of this at all and clearly hated me. She said her class was full. I said I'd bring my own chair into class. She said there was no space. I said I'd sit outside the door. Her final excuse was that it was almost the end of the year, I had missed out on all the teaching so far and would 'lower her class average'. I had no choice but to remain in the science stream. However, I took economics as an additional subject. A sixth subject. I studied the entire year's course in three days and gave the final exam. Our exam papers did not have names on them, only roll numbers. When I got my paper, I found I had got 76 marks out of 100. The highest that year was 79. I barged into Mrs Sharma's class, my paper in hand, and threw it on her desk with the words, 'Here's your average'. I wish I still had balls like that!

What I have retained from that sixteen-year-old is the spirit of rebellion. If someone tells me there is something I am not capable of doing, or is impossible to do, I will put all my energy into ensuring I bloody well do it. I'm quite mature like that! Also, my method of protest is to try and do the job as brilliantly as it can possibly be done. I may not succeed, but I do try. As Steve Martin said, be so good that they can't ignore you.

I was quite a star student in school. I came first in my class in class six, seven, eight, nine, ten and twelve. In class eleven, I was not eligible because I was in Canada for one term. But I was not academically inclined at all. I didn't really study much. Also, at the time, glory didn't lie in academics. It lay in sport. While I was always a very skinny kid, I was super fit. I may not have been very strong, but I had an insane amount of stamina, above-average hand-eye coordination, and I was quick on my feet. As a sixteen-year-old, I could run three kilometres in under ten and a half minutes and I could also do one hundred metres in twelve seconds. As a result, I was on a lot of the school teams— cricket, football, field hockey, athletics, cross country and table tennis. The only two sports I didn't pick up were swimming and tennis. I even tried my hand at boxing. While I won a couple of bouts in school, when I went for district-level matches, I was handed a thorough beating by a young vegetable vendor called Pinku. I am not likely to ever forget that name!

The other district-level tournament I clearly remember was played in a town called Bilaspur. The entire hockey team travelled from school by the local bus and must have been on it for ten hours at least. Exhausted, we crashed as soon as we reached our destination. The following day, we played quite well and won most of our matches. As a reward, our coach allowed us the evening off.

Instead of roaming the town after dinner, the bunch of us went in search of a video parlour that screened porn. We found it in a dark and dingy basement and sat for half an hour, our heads covered by shawls, until the parlour closed. When the final film finished playing and the lights were turned on, we discovered our hockey coach sitting in the rear corner of the room with a shawl wrapped around his head!

We didn't get a firing that night. I'm guessing because he really wasn't in a position to point the finger at anyone. However, we did get a dressing-down after we lost our matches the next day. The coach didn't think we had spent our time at the tournament in the most 'appropriate' way.

Hockey coach apart, we had some interesting teachers in senior school. There was an accounts teacher who never understood why it wasn't okay to say, 'Please, open the window and let the air force come in'. Until one day, when a student responded, 'Sir, why don't we open the tap and let the navy come out?'

I still remember this teacher's speech to the class eleven batch at their first ever accountancy elective class. It went something like this: 'Accountancy is the very important profession. Imagine I am a shopkeeper in the Garkhal city. [Garkhal was a village down the road from our school. It was literally one lane, with a few shops on each side. Calling Garkhal a city was like calling the Vatican City a solar system.] At the end of the year, if I finish my accounts and the chartered accountant signs on it, even the chief minister cannot say anything! Also, you can give the chartered accountancy examination fourteen times. They hold no grudge. I myself failed only twelve times!'

We had a teacher called Dr D.C. Gupta, who was called 'Chappu'. He used to threaten to slap you so hard that it would leave fingerprints on your face. The way he said it was, 'I put the slap, fingers stay, hand come back!' Soon, everyone in school with the surname Gupta was being called Chappu.

You know how nicknames are made up in school. right? They are usually just a bastardisation of your name. At Sanawar, though, the kids would try and tease you with different names. And the second you showed your irritation with one of them, that would be the name that stuck. Also, there were some names that were inherited if you had a sibling in school. For example, there was a guy who possessed an ample bosom and was nicknamed 'Pom Pom'. When his younger brother joined, he was called 'Chut Pom Pom' ('chut' is slang for small) and since they were in school at the same time, Pom Pom became Big Pom Pom. The funny thing about nicknames is that eventually you forget the real name of the person. Even twenty years later, when you meet people from school, you only know them by their nicknames, even if their breasts have grown smaller!

We had a teacher called Saina Mukherjee. She taught geography and was housemistress for one of the girls' houses. I remember one night, when three of us broke into the swimming-pool complex. Since we didn't have costumes handy, we went skinny dipping. A short while later, Ms Saina was passing the pool area. She peeped in through the window and reprimanded us severely for breaking rules and being there at 10 p.m. at night. We apologised profusely. She asked us to get out immediately. And of course we responded by saying, 'Sorry ma'am, we cannot'. It took about thirty seconds for her to figure it out and walk away, leaving us with our tiny dignities.

We also had a teacher called Mr B. Singh. He had a magnificent moustache and was obviously referred to as Muchchu. He was the deputy headmaster of the school and also by far the most revered and feared member of faculty. He served the school for forty-two years and raised generations of Sanawarians. The school as we knew it was built by him. You could time your watch by his footsteps. We knew at what time he would step into which classroom when doing his rounds. When I say 'we' knew, I mean the whole school, except for my good friend Harpreet.

One evening, at prep time, Harpreet was reading a 'pondi'. Nowdays, of course, teenagers surf porn on their mobile phones. And the range of magazines available is vast. Not to mention the variety of porn stars. For my generation, it was Samantha Fox, the woman who taught us what breasts were. You show me a man born between 1972 and 1982 and I'll show you a man who has wanked off to a Sam Fox poster!

The pondis we were able to procure in boarding school were of two kinds. One kind, like the popular *Debonair*, carried pictures of topless women. They could have been the ugliest women in the world, but they were topless and that was all that mattered. Nobody was looking at their faces. The second type of pondis contained erotic stories that could be read; the most popular of these was called *Human Digest*. Now, in a boarding school in those days, a pornographic magazine was like gold dust. You never got an entire magazine. You got one page. And if you were lucky, it was a good part!

So, anyway, one day, my friend Harpreet had one page of an HD tucked inside his text book. While he was engrossed in his literary pursuits, Mr B. Singh walked up behind him and tapped him on the shoulder. Harpreet turned around and looked at Muchchu, who was signalling to him to pass the piece of paper. At ninja speed, which is to say a split second at most, Harpreet turned around, crumpled up the paper and ate it up! I guess the equivalent would be a modern-day teenager swallowing his mobile phone. And trust me, the mobile phone would not have been around as much as that piece of paper had been around!

Remember, the internet had just come to India in the mid-1990s. And we didn't have speeds that allowed us to download videos. At best, we could download photographs. And I still remember how those used to load. First you had the hair, then you had the eyes, then you got the nose.... by this point, eighteen minutes had gone by and you were only getting warmed up. In one corner, you could hear the modem going kree-kroo-kree-kroo. Even today, when I hear the sound of a modem, I get turned on!

Mr B. Singh retired the year before I became head boy. His wife, the kind and lovely Mrs B. Singh, remained as matron for the eleventh and twelfth dormitories. She loved us boys dearly, but wasn't a fan of the girls. She didn't hold back from showing her displeasure either, half-jokingly and half-seriously, towards those boys who spent time with girls!

Then, in May 1994, we received news of Mr B. Singh's sudden demise. A bunch of us students and faculty piled into a bus to go attend his funeral in Palampur. When we returned at 11 p.m., I went to the then deputy headmaster, Mr C.B. Abraham, to ask him what the protocol would be for the official school mourning the next day. To my utter shock and dismay, he said there would be none. I could not understand it. I remembered the official mourning when Mr Batish had died a few years earlier and could not see why the school would not do the same thing in honour of the most revered man in the school's 147-year history. I argued with Mr Abraham, but he would not budge. That night, I decided that whether or not the faculty supported it, the students would do what was required of them in Mr B. Singh's memory. I sent messages out to all the school prefects that the school would observe mourning the next day.

The time for morning PT went by without incident. The staff understood and left the students alone. The students did not carry their books up for classes. There was usually one class held before breakfast. At breakfast, a class seven student informed me that a faculty member had given them a test. I asked him how it had gone. He said all the boys had turned in blank papers. I asked him what the girls had done and he said they had submitted blank papers as well. My heart filled with pride at the courage of these twelve-year-olds. I told him I'd have a word with the teacher. However, before lunch, a bunch of class twelve students had already gone to the new member of faculty and offered to chop his testicles off, leading him to make the counter offer of considering the test cancelled and not failing any of the students.

Breakfast that day was followed by assembly. By now, the faculty were aware of what the students were doing. After assembly, the deputy headmaster stood next to me and instructed a bunch of thirteen-year-olds to go and get their books. Not one of them moved. Mr Abraham told me to tell them, and I refused. The faculty then held a few meetings after which I, along with the prefects, was called to meet the headmaster and other senior teachers. I remember the meeting like it was yesterday. I was asked who was responsible for the 'strike'. I said that I was. I was asked if I was aware that I could be thrown out of school for this. I said I was. When asked why I did it, I said that if the faculty did not have the decency to pay their respects to a man who dedicatedly served the school for forty-two years, then the students would do it themselves. A dramatic altercation followed, and it was agreed that there would be no classes that day, and an official school mourning would be held in Mr B. Singh's honour, but the students would have to go and get their books right away (I'm guessing so the faculty could be seen to be 'winning').

That Sunday, a remembrance service was held in school and over 2000 past students made their way up the mountain to pay their respects to their teacher who was no more.

There was another time when my student's code of honour was severely tested. That night, in early 1995, I was called to Mr Abraham's house. He told me that some boys had gone to the girls' dormitory and while he knew who they were, he needed me to confirm their names. I told him that I had been in the school for nine years and while I did not know their names, I was surprised he expected me to actually tell him who they were. He warned me that there were significant awards coming my way and that if I didn't tell him the names, I'd lose those. I didn't budge, and neither did he. I did, of course, know the name of every single boy who had gone to the girls' dormitory. But when you grow up with a code, you honour that code. Maybe that's why *Scent of a Woman* remains my favourite film. Maybe secretly I wish that I had an Al Pacino or Colonel Frank Slade speaking in my defence: 'I can tell you this: he won't sell anybody out to buy his future. And that, my friends, is called integrity. That's called courage. Now, that's the stuff leaders should be made of.'

I really did want to end this chapter with the previous paragraph, to make me look good. However, I did once tattle on somebody. In fact, one of my closest friends. During the class twelve board exams, my friend KD (Ketan) wasn't really putting in the kind of effort he should have been. So, on the sly, I called up his father in Calcutta and told him to fire KD, without of course revealing the source of his information. I happened to be with KD when he was called to his housemaster's residence to take the call. He came out crying and deeply upset about the dressing-down his father had given him. Being the good friend I was, instead of telling him his father was right, I said, 'Don't worry, bro. You'll be fine.' Face palm.

But KD did start to focus a little bit more on his studies. So much so that he decided to break up with his girlfriend. Since he was so focussed on his lessons, I was assigned the responsibility of writing the break-up letter. It was pretty standard format. You're a lovely girl, this isn't going to work out, I hope we can still be friends. The usual. Yes, ALL men are bastards, we ALL say the same things and yes, it's not you, it's us!

The three most important days on our school calendar were around Founders' Day: 2–4 October. That's when the alumni and the parents came up to school and we got to showcase our skills. The athletics meet, the NCC parade, Tattoo, bugle band, mass PT, sports matches against the alumni…the works. One of the downsides of being in a boarding school is that your parents don't get to share your everyday victories. They don't get to see you act in a play or win a race, or be witness to any of your achievements while they are actually taking place. They only get news of it afterwards. And that's not the same thing.

Founders' Day in class twelve was something I had been looking forward to for a long time. I was head boy of the school. I was the NCC parade commander, and we had been training for months. I had a lead role in the school play. I was the school athletics captain and 3000 m champ, which meant I'd be carrying the torch to light the flame at the athletics meet. I was in the bugle band and leading mass PT. This really was my moment of glory. And it was an opportunity for me to perform in front of my parents. An opportunity that I had long waited for.

I played the clarinet in the school band for six years

Taking the oath while leading the annual school athletics meet

Except, that's not how it turned out. In September that year, there was an outbreak of bubonic and pneumonic plague in south-central and south-western India. Rumour had it that our headmaster, who had been schooled at a rival school, was afraid of dealing with some of the questions that were likely to be thrown his way by the alumni during the meeting on Founders' Day. So, using the plague as an excuse, he shut down the school on 10 October. No amount of persuasion could change his mind. Parents weren't even allowed to step into the school campus, and we had to pack our bags and go home. The rest of the term was cancelled. We were to return only for our end-of-year exams.

It broke my heart. Nine years of anticipation had built up to this. I could feel it, smell it, almost taste it. I had worked my ass off for it. But with one man's snap decision, it was all gone. I can't remember studying for my board exams even for a day after getting back home. In fact, our teachers hadn't even been able to complete the syllabus. Two months after the exams, my housemaster called me to let me know that the winner of the Chief of Army Staff's Medal for the best all-rounder had been decided. I had lost out by one point. Why? Because one of the deciding factors was the teachers' vote. One point was allotted for each vote and as head boy I received nine votes and the boy who won got fifty-two.

This was an award I had aspired to since the day I joined school. I had school spirit flowing through my veins. But I didn't feel as much pain as I expected to when I heard the news. You can't break a heart that has already been broken. While I felt comforted on hearing the words of two of my favourite teachers, Mrs Khan and Mr K.J. Parel, both of whom said to me that the students loved me because they knew I'd always stood up for them, the fact was that nine wonderful years of schooling ended on a bitter note.

In the head boy's room, with students from the batch just below mine

I didn't walk away from school with that medal, but I did walk away with a set of values that formed the very core of my being. Including a healthy disregard for both rules and positions of authority that had not proven their worth, and a strong sense of right and wrong that had to be defended and stood up for, no matter the cost. This realisation dawned on me in 2019 when, out of the blue, my housemaster from class nine, Mr Soham Anand (whose signature I can forge even today!) wrote a Facebook post about an incident that had taken place twenty-six years earlier. An incident that I had long forgotten.

He wrote:

A Page from My Diary
Sanawar 1993
Lesson in Courage and Humility

Some memories keep coming back, too strong to be blown away, needs expression, can't put it out of my mind.

The year was 1993. The day Diwali.

With the setting of the sun and darkness descending, the Seniors had departed for Peace Stead, for what they called real excitement, for boys and girls mingled together freely to celebrate Diwali, the sight of which I had never seen or experienced before. Crackers worth thousands of rupees are reduced to ash and smoke in no time.

I held myself back to be with the Juniors to celebrate a more sedate Diwali, who otherwise hesitate going to PS and being with the Seniors.

A rocket fired by a junior lost its track and direction, not only hit me on my palm, but got glued for a good minute or so before it could be disengaged, leaving my palm in a mess of melting flesh and blood with third degree burns, and hand numb with burning pain.

Repeated calls to the RMO (Resident Medical Officer) did not evoke much response, she too was out, so was rest of the supporting staff.

CJ got to know about the incident and rushed to my residence. Just then a parent, Doctor by profession, Dr Walia dropped in to meet his son, Chiteshwar Walia, now practising medicine. He examined my palm and advised immediate medical attention, which was not available, nor could have been made available, what with the hospital shut and time close to 8.00 pm.

Nevertheless Dr Walia gently cleaned the wound with whatever first aid was available at home and loosely covered it with a muslin cloth to avoid exposure and infection, wrote a lengthy prescription along with do's and don'ts, instructing me to get it first thing in the morning, which I carefully kept under a paper weight on the piano top.

After Dr Walia left, I sat down with a stiff drink to ease the pain. My wife from the kitchen shouted, not to forget to get onions tomorrow, we've run out of them.

CJ, all this while, watching and listening intently, left saying he'll be back shortly.

Indeed he was back, within less than an hour, breathless, red in the face, but with a broad grin on his face and a mischievous twinkle in his eyes, his outstretched hands holding two bags. One he gave to my wife, the other to me. One had onions, the other medicines.

Both me and my wife were left speechless. We looked at each other for what looked like a long time, but not more than a few seconds. I could clearly see a look of blankness on my wife's face. Time just stood still, hard to describe the feelings I was going through, completely tongue tied. I didn't really know how to say what I wanted to say. There was a lot I wanted to say, but there remained a lot that went unsaid. Both of us were swept off our feet, trying to hold back the tears on the verge of rolling down the eyes.

Apparently, CJ made a short cut, running down the hill side from the Lower Barne Field and up the hill to Kasauli, to avoid being detected, forcing the chemist to open the store, picking up onions from the vegetable vendor, making his way back the same route, all in less than an hour.

He missed his dinner.

'You broke bounds, CJ,' I finally muttered. 'Yes, maybe,' he replied, 'but all for a good cause.'

What could I possibly call this!

The loveliest masterpiece of God is a heart full of love. He certainly does have one. Beauty, truth and goodness, as it is said are the three most valuable virtues. CJ, I think, has all of them and has them in abundance. He did teach me that evening a lesson or two in what it means to be beyond self and humble.

There is something very open and generous about him and it is his generosity which makes him what he today is.

It was an encounter with gentleness, humility and love.

For twenty-six years I had carried the burden of losing the Chief of Army Staff's Medal in my heart. But I'll take this Facebook post over any medal every single day of the week. And twice on a Sunday.

With Mr Soham Anand

a tale of two cities

By the end of my schooling, I had a file as thick as the Magna Carta, filled with certificates of achievement. However, given I had spent nine years studying on a mountain top in the middle of nowhere, I had very little understanding of the real world. And because I had always excelled at everything I touched, my parents never felt the need to give me a pep talk. As a result, I didn't realise the importance of academics. To be more specific, I didn't realise how important the class twelve board exams were. I had always topped my class with very little effort and I didn't see how the board exams could be any different. I was in for a rude shock.

My parents were considering a move to Delhi at the time. Therefore, I decided to apply to colleges in Delhi University. As I waited for the board exam results to be published, the subject that I was most nervous about was computer science—I had barely understood a single question in that exam. In the end, in addition to answering the little that I knew, I had written Lord Ram's name at the top of every single answer sheet and prayed that my paper would not be marked by an examiner who professed faith in a different religion. On the last page of my answer sheet I also wrote an impassioned account of how I was the first person in my family to go to school and had four unmarried younger sisters to support whose lives would be ruined if I didn't go to college and get a good job. The best marks I got were in computer science.

In spite of my 'excellent' computer brain, I had attained an average of seventy-six per cent across my top four subjects. My entire education was built on a philosophy of all-round development, but suddenly, when it came to college admissions, it all boiled down to one piece of paper—the class twelve mark sheet. I'd carry my thick file of certificates for college admissions and it wouldn't even merit a look. It was like everything that I was led to believe was pure and good and true meant nothing at all. One by one, every single college rejected me. I felt the way Leonardo Di Caprio must have felt at the Oscars every year. (He finally has one now after years of being nominated and not winning.) I felt the way L.K. Advani must have felt when Narendra Modi became prime minister—all those years of waiting and looking forward to the best years of your life, only to have them taken away just when the time seemed right.

Having failed the academic entrance requirements, I started trying to qualify for college admission via sport. I went for every sports trial possible. Cricket, football, athletics...and I was let down each time. Firstly, by the system, for it seemed that no matter how talented you were, unless you knew someone who knew the right people, you could not get in. Secondly, by my own abilities. It turned out that being the fastest runner in a school in the mountains didn't translate very well when competing on a track in the middle of the Delhi summer. I lost more sweat running 200 m in Delhi than I had running 3000 m in school.

Given my abilities in track and field were not up to the mark, I decided to take the battle indoors. I was the chess champion of my school and of Solan district. I had also got to the Himachal state finals against an opponent I was assured of beating, thereby qualifying for the nationals. As it happened, on the Sunday that the finals were to be held, I had a date in school and I had been assured 'action'. The expectation that had been set was third base—if you're unfamiliar with the term, I won't explain it to you, but please accept my condolences.

For a sixteen-year-old, it was not a difficult decision to make. I faked illness that morning and refused to get into the van to go to Shimla. I did not become state champion. I was not invited to the nationals. But yes, though I did not get to say 'check' that day, I did get to mate. And yes, that is the level of punning I am willing to stoop to and this was not the last time my libido clouded my better judgment.

But I digress. Back to the story. I applied for chess trials at Hindu College and went on to defeat a national-level player. After the match, we had to walk to an office in a different building to record the result. That's when I was introduced to Delhi entitlement as my eighteen-year-old opponent issued his threat—'*Bol de ki main ne jeeta hai varna tujhe marwa doonga. Tu jaanta nahi mera baap kaun hai.*' (You better tell them that I won the match, otherwise I'll get you killed. You don't know who my father is.) To which I responded—'*Tu kuch bhi kar le. Yeh match toh main ne hee jeeta hai.'* (You can do what you like. I won this match.) After the torture I had been through, I was inclined to take my chances with this pipsqueak rather than lose my only chance to get into college.

Then Hindu College informed me that since I had got in through the sports quota, I could choose any course I wanted besides a bachelor's in economics (honours) and commerce. While a bachelor's in commerce is what I wanted to pursue, I had no choice but to pick another course if I wanted to go to college. Not only did I have no choice, I also had no understanding of what a lot of the other courses were about and how they might help me in the future. As a result, to 'keep my options open', I opted for a bachelor's in electronics (honours). At that time, the choice of degree was determined less by what one enjoyed or was good at, and more by what one thought would increase the chances of getting a job after college. I attended a sum total of one class during my entire undergraduate career. I walked into a class where eighty-nine per cent was the second lowest board exam score (the lowest was mine) and people were reading books like *Physics Is Fun*...out of choice! I knew immediately that this was not for me.

Since the B.Sc gig wasn't really working, I dropped out of college and took up a course in B.Com (honours) by correspondence. This was the equivalent of a distance-learning programme. I would only need to be in Delhi to appear for my exams and would eventually get a degree from the University of Delhi. Since my parents' move to Delhi hadn't worked out, this meant that my life for the next two years would be split between two cities, Delhi and Calcutta.

The Delhi experience was unique. The company that my father worked for had bought a two-storey building which they had converted into a hostel. It was meant for the children of those employees who had come to Delhi to pursue their education. The ground floor had the dining area, a kitchen, a table tennis table, a small library, a TV room, a common room, and the warden's office. The first floor was the boys' floor and the second floor was the girls'. There were between two and five students in each room. The hostel was centrally air-conditioned and we would be given three meals a day. By the standards of anyone going to college in India, this was a life of luxury.

Of course, not everything worked in those days. We would have long power outages in the middle of summer when no fans or air coolers would work. We had to invent methods of staying alive when temperatures soared above forty-five degrees centigrade. One method was to soak your bedsheet in cold water (the water that comes from the 'cold' water taps in the Delhi summer is almost boiling hot), spread the sheet across the bed and lie absolutely still on top of it in only your underwear while enjoying the little breeze that drifted in from outside. I say breeze, but what we got was a combination of the Delhi loo (the loo is the warm wind that blows in the summer) and the exhaust from the restaurants in the market that our hostel was situated behind.

Our second method of staying cool, especially during exams, was by visiting a fast-food restaurant called Wimpy's. They had an outlet at M Block Market in Greater Kailash Part 1 and our hostel was just behind it. The strategy heads of the Wimpy's conglomerate had come up with a wonderful marketing campaign that they thought would help their business flourish. If you bought a soft drink or an aerated beverage, you could get unlimited refills that same day. Now, this might have been a successful promotion in other parts of the world. However, the powers that be at the Wimpy's empire had clearly underestimated the students of Goodricke Hostel. Our capacity for exploiting loopholes in a promotion could have brought down the Roman Empire at the height of its power—had Caeser been offering free drinks to thirsty students in the Delhi summer. We would go to Wimpy's in the morning after breakfast, order a cola, and sit there for eight hours. This allowed us to study in air-conditioned comfort during long power cuts and drink the weight of a small elephant in soft drinks over the course of the day, all for the price of one cola. It took less than one profitable quarter for Wimpy's to discontinue the promotion.

Since most children whose parents worked in a tea company had quite a sheltered upbringing, it was quite easy for our young, impressionable minds to be swept away by the sprawling metropolis that was Delhi. Also, for the first time, I was out of the strict regimen of a boarding school. I grew my hair long, started wearing an assortment of beads around my neck and took a liking for bandanas. Once, a day or two before Holi (the festival of colours), an aunt who lived in Delhi suggested that I consider getting a haircut. The next day, I went and shaved my head. Teenage rebellion and issues with authority clearly hadn't left my side yet!

I learnt in the weeks to follow that, as a bald man, if you don't take the right precautions or play with the wrong

Holi colours, you will have the head of an exotic parrot for many days to follow. I also remember (faintly, of course) all of us trying *bhang* during Holi. If you're not familiar with bhang, it is basically an edible preparation of cannabis. The buds and leaves of cannabis are ground into a paste, which is often mixed with milk and drunk. That fateful Holi, when we first-timers didn't know that it took a while for the effects of bhang to kick in and therefore had a glass or two too many, many adventures took place. One boy climbed to the terrace and proclaimed his love for the girl in the house next door on a loudspeaker. Another thought he was drowning while 'swimming' on the cement floor. My friend Parakram and I went to the washroom to take a leak and stood at the urinal for twenty minutes. God only knows what kind of conversation we had for that long, with our members in our hands.

I should state for the record that I've never been enamoured by, or attracted to, any form of drugs. I never had bhang again and while I've been in many situations where friends were doing lines of cocaine and offered me one, I've always said no. And I've never tried any other drugs. No ecstasy, heroine, marijuana, MDMA or whatever else is out there. But I've also never judged people who use them. Many of them are wonderful and incredibly kind people and how they choose to live their lives is their choice. To each their own. A bourbon and cola will do me just fine.

Our hostel warden in Delhi, Satish Talwar (or as he pronounced it, S'teesh), was constantly under pressure. Almost every person in the hostel was dating someone and while members of the opposite sex from outside the hostel were not allowed in our rooms, we often found ways to distract the security guard and sneak someone up. S'teesh shouted at us and told us that we were turning the place into a warehouse. We were all very confused by this accusation. It was much later that we understood that 'warehouse' was what he thought the pronunciation of 'whorehouse' was. And then we couldn't help wondering which was the greater crime—sleeping with someone of the opposite sex with their consent or screwing an entire language without the language's consent!

A bald me with Vikram on the extreme right

S'teesh would often gatecrash hostel parties hoping he might get a glimpse of the place when it was transformed into the warehouse he had been led to believe it was. He was never successful in his attempts. Each time something went wrong at the hostel, his method of solving the crime and discovering the guilty party was to randomly walk up to a resident and accuse them with the line—'You are the one'. As soon as the student denied the accusation, he'd respond with, 'Okay, then tell me who is the one'. Sherlock Holmes would have been proud of such superlative abilities of deduction. Sadly for S'teesh, I guess what they say is true: You might spend your whole life searching and still never find 'the one'.

One of the naughty things we did at the hostel was to mess with the minds of students who had just joined. Not everyone was in college; some were still in high school. I remember one boy who joined the hostel when he was in class eleven. In the course of two hours, we convinced him, one after another, that his future lay in six different professions. By the end of it, he wanted to join the army! Then there was this young boy who started dating a girl three years older than him; she was in her second year of college. Every afternoon, they would 'retire to her chambers' and we'd hear Barry White songs blasting through the hostel corridors. We could only assume she was giving him advanced tuitions.

It turned out that the subjects he was studying in class eleven were English, physics, chemistry, mathematics and computer science. Three times a week, an external tutor would give him extra classes in physics, chemistry, mathematics and computer science—all his subjects excluding English. At the end of the school year, he had scored 87 marks out of 500. Of those, 70 were in English. In the other subjects for which he had taken tutions for the entire year, he got an average of

4.25 per cent. His mother immediately withdrew him from the hostel and took him back to the tea gardens of Assam… and he had Barry White to thank for that.

I wasn't the sharpest tool in the box myself. In my first year of college, I got a first division, but my marks in accountancy were not so good. I had never studied the subject before and found it very confusing. By the second year, I was more focussed on having fun than studying. One time, in the middle of exams, I convinced my friend Parakram that we should take a short golfing holiday in Shimla. Parakram wasn't madly keen, so we tossed a coin. I won the toss and off we went. We came back just in time for our company law examination. When the final results came in, I had failed in two subjects and got a sum total of forty per cent. Had I got half a mark less, I would have failed the year. I considered sending my paper for re-evaluation, but was scared that if they adjusted my marks downward, I'd have to repeat the year. Parakram was not as fortunate and had to repeat the second year. It's been over twenty years now, but I still haven't had the heart to tell him that the subject that caused him to fail, company law, was the one I received my highest marks in that year.

That year, I also gave my first year accountancy paper again, with the intention of improving my scores of the past year. Since I was doing a distance learning degree and didn't have a fixed college, I was assigned a different examination centre for every paper. The examiner, therefore, did not know my name or my face and all that I wrote was my roll number on the examination paper. My strategy was simple. I wore running shoes and sat at the desk closest to the doorway. My plan was to glance through the exam paper as soon as I received it. If it looked like I would do well, I would sit and finish the exam. If I thought the paper was tough, I'd make a run for it. I had paid an auto-rickshaw driver some money to wait by the main gate for twenty minutes. I'd get into the rickshaw and disappear before the examiner knew what was happening. Luckily for me, the paper seemed very simple and I was confident I'd score above ninety per cent, if not a perfect hundred. When the results came, my average for the first year had dropped because I had failed that paper too. And I didn't even have the pleasure of Barry White's company every afternoon.

I remember two other instances of causing anguish to friends. One had to do with a friend who had a very thick moustache. One night, a few students (notice I'm not saying a few of 'us' because I still feel that what happened was wrong), sneaked into his bedroom and shaved off half his moustache. Notice, I said shaved and not trimmed. He was such a heavy sleeper, they were able to shave him. Also notice I said half his moustache. To be precise, only the left side of his face was shaved. The next morning, we tried hard to control our laughter when he came down for breakfast without a moustache. One of the boys asked him, 'Bro, how come you shaved off your moustache?' He replied, 'I was brushing my teeth this morning and saw black black stuff coming out. And when I washed my face, I saw my moustache had fallen off!' We burst into laughter.

We had a wonderful neighbour, two houses down, by the name of Vikram. He was a fun guy and built like a truck.

We took it upon ourselves to become his career counsellors. Vikram was just finishing school and wasn't sure what he would like to study in college. We convinced him that the Indian education system would not appreciate his 'unique talents and personality' and that his future lay on foreign shores. Inspired by our pep talk, Vikram went home and told his father that he wanted to study abroad. His father, being an army man, told him bluntly that he didn't have the money to pay for a foreign education and that he would have to make do in India.

When Vikram came back and told us this, we convinced him that he was a genius and that American universities would bend over backwards to give him a full scholarship, and therefore all he needed was money for the SATs. He went back home and reported this to his father, who clearly had a better understanding of his son's abilities and swiftly told Vikram to fuck right off. Vikram came to us, dejected. We said, don't worry lad, we'll find a way. Vikram had received a tennis racket as a birthday present only recently. The cost of the racket would cover the fee payable for SAT. Egged on by us, Vikram stood in the middle of the market for over three hours, trying to sell his racket to random passers-by. When that failed, we went to a sports store called Rio Grand in the market, which offered him one-sixth the price of the racket. He returned disappointed and eventually joined the Delhi College of Arts and Commerce. I'm pleased to say that he is currently a successful motivational speaker and team-building coach and his 'unique talents and personality' are much appreciated in his chosen line of work. Oh, but what might have been had he made it abroad!

*Soumya receives birthday bumps at the hostel from Parakram,
Imran and Barry White!*

The Calcutta experience was quite different to Delhi. I
enjoyed being back there as an eighteen-year-old. Calcutta
is a warm and welcoming city. I had made a few friends
during my visits back from school and their social circles
let me in. And since college years are the time for mischief,
that is exactly what we got up to. I remember going out at
night with black shoe polish and a brush when an All India
Congress Conference was in progress, and applying my
creative skills to some of the posters featuring politicians.
The next day, when my friend Chetan was driving with his
father, he pointed at one such poster of a politician who had
magically put on a pair of sunglasses and grown a Hitler
moustache overnight. Chetan said to his father, 'Daddy,
look what somebody did.' Yash uncle, who knew us all too

well, responded immediately, 'Rascal! When did you people do this?' Art appreciation obviously wasn't his thing.

There was an even more fun part of the Congress Conference. The political party had put life-size cardboard cut-outs of politicians all over the city. One such cut-out was that of a politician by the name of Sitaram Kesri. He had the face of a toad and was the size of…well, a toad. I exaggerate, of course: he was maybe five feet tall. Chetan and I stole one such cardboard cut-out and carried it back to his house. We took Mr Kesri into the kitchen, shut the door, hid in a corner, and waited. Nelu Aunty, Chetan's mother, was an early riser. At 5 a.m., eyes half closed, she opened the kitchen door to see Mr Sitaram Kesri, arms folded, standing right in front of her, saying namaste. She screamed and went running out into the garden. We had the laugh of a lifetime, followed by the dressing-down of a lifetime.

As it turned out, the morning's histrionics were not yet done. At 6 a.m., as Chetan's father was going out for his morning walk, Chetan's brother Varun got back home after a night of partying. We could hear Yash uncle admonishing him: 'Bloody fool. When I told you to come home early, I didn't mean early in the morning!'

Two of the nuttiest friends in that magic circle of mine were Nicky and Ricky. Once, they were driving an Ambassador. As the car headed towards a crossing, Ricky calmly said to Nicky, 'Nicky, the brakes have failed. What should we do?' 'Let's jump into the back seat,' said Nicky. Both boys leaped into the back seat of the car and adopted the brace position that is advised on aircrafts in anticipation of a crash. The car hurtled towards the crossing and crashed into the back of a taxi. Luckily, nobody was hurt. The taxi driver, in a rage, came running to their car to pick a fight. He opened the door on the driver's side, ready to throw a punch, and to his surprise, found nobody there. He looked in the back to see Nicky and Ricky still in brace position. Ricky looked up at him and said most earnestly, 'Sorry, bhaiya. Brakes failed.' The taxi driver burst into laughter.

I drove a Maruti Gypsy in those days. It was the car my father taught me how to drive in, in the back streets of the area that we lived in. In those days, you could either give a driving test or, for a small fee, have your driving licence home delivered. The fries were free if it came fifteen minutes late. I'm joking, of course. The cut off was thirty minutes.

I, however, chose to give my driving test (as I'd like to categorically state for legal reasons). My friend Chetan, a keen auto enthusiast, helped me make a few changes to my mini-SUV. (Side note: Chetan was very careful with his own cars but when he drove anyone else's, it was like he was in a Formula One race in an indestructible monster truck. The car's tyres were bound to lose a few years by the time he was done with it.) The first major bit of work we did to the Gypsy was to put big rally-driving halogen lights in the front. The second thing we did was to remove the silencer from the exhaust and replace it with a one-box, so each time you accelerated, there would be a very loud noise. And the third thing we did was to replace the car's horn with an old vintage car hooter that was loud beyond imagination. The lights and the hooter were sourced from Calcutta's infamous chor bazaar, which literally means thieves' market. It was where you went to buy stolen parts. Urban legend has it that a man in a Mercedes went to buy a hub cap for his car. The man who sold it to him stalled the buyer by telling him that his boy was going to get it from a room at the back. The boy, meanwhile, went to the buyer's car, stole a hub cap off it, and sold it back to him. Such was the nature of chor bazaar.

Armed with my customised mean machine, my friends and I initiated a campaign that Prime Minister Narendra Modi has been publicising in the recent past—Swachh Bharat (clean India). Late at night, we would drive down the by-lanes of Calcutta very slowly, with the lights off. The second we spotted a man urinating on the side of the road, our car would sneak up close to him and then, all at once, the bright halogen lights would focus on him, the silencer would roar, and the hooter would…hoot. Very loudly. We've had men running a 100 m dash with penis in hand as the vehicle of death chased them down the road. I realise now it was a mean thing to do, but it was very funny for us at the time. And we were doing our civic duty by keeping pee off the walls.

Once, when mum and dad were travelling, I went to park the Gypsy in the basement parking lot. I was taking a sharp turn in when—too late—I saw the oil on the ground. The vehicle skidded and went straight into a pillar. Dad was in Poland at the time, so I called him to inform him of the accident. After ensuring that I was not hurt, he asked what the damage was. I told him the bull bar at the front was smashed, the radiator was leaking, and the wheels didn't turn properly. He consoled me and said not to worry about it and that when he was young he had once driven his car into a train. Sorry, WHAT! I didn't say that out loud, but I did wonder, how on earth could anyone drive a car into a train?

There was another occasion when dad's response to a situation was quite different from anything one might accept. I was sixteen years old and mum was travelling. Dad normally came home from office at 6.30 p.m. sharp. Since there was nobody home, a 'special friend' (as my parents' generation might call someone of the opposite sex in whom one's interest wasn't purely platonic) and I were fooling around in dad's room late in the afternoon. For the record, she was above eighteen. Now, dad decided that since his son was alone, he would come home early. So, in he walks, to find his bedroom door locked. He knocks, and I come out and ask him to sit in the drawing room. This is how the conversation went.

CJ: Dad, there is a girl inside.

Dad: So, what is she doing?

I was sixteen and couldn't think of anything fast enough. So I decided to go with the truth.

CJ: She's just putting her clothes on.

Dad: What! This is how you get into alcohol and drugs and all.

In my head I'm thinking, how on earth is that even related!

Dad: So I presume she is leaving now?

CJ: Yes, of course. But if you don't mind, could you please go to the balcony and look the other way?

My father kindly obliged, and she left. I don't think my father ever told my mother about this and he only brought the incident up once, much later. It was the following year and I was to come home from school to an empty house. He said, 'You know, last time you brought a girl home. I hope you won't do that this time.' I said, 'No dad, I won't.' And that was that.

Talking about alcohol and drugs, another incident comes to mind, involving my friend Raju. Drunk out of his skull, he drove the wrong way down a one-way Park Street at night. It was sometime around Christmas. The police sergeant pulled him over and started to pull out his pad to write a ticket. Raju then put forth his eloquent defence: 'Sir. You are Bengali. I am Bengali. Please let me go. It's Christmas.' The sergeant, after reprimanding him, actually let him go without a ticket. That is, until Raju carried on driving the wrong way!

We had two main watering holes in those days. The first was a pub called 'Someplace Else', which we fondly referred to as 'some other place'. It was at the Park Hotel on Park Street. Once or twice a month, that's where everyone would go. It was essentially a pub the size of a large living room, with a long bar and a tiny dance floor at one end. When they had live music, the band would position itself at the end of the rectangular room and people would dance in any space they could find. The only other famous night spot in Calcutta was a disco called The Pink Elephant. 'The Pink' was at the Oberoi Hotel and had been around for many years. We didn't go there because it was the party spot for the generation above ours. Also, yes, in those days they were called 'discos'. It's what people call nightclubs now, but discos were way cooler. Mostly because we had better music. You see, our music had something some young people might not be familiar with. They are called lyrics. Actual words within a song. Shocking, right?

A wonderful young man by the name of Anirban Simlai would sit at a desk at the entrance of Someplace Else. He always kept in front of him a bowl of sweets that he allowed us to dip into freely. He was responsible for collecting the entrance fee for going into Someplace Else. Given the size of the place, most people actually hung out outside the club, in the lobby of the hotel. They would dip in for a beer and then step out because most people were hanging out in the lobby anyway. It's like that film, *A Night at Roxbury*, where in effect the club is outside the club! I almost never went inside, because I felt that the price was too high: ₹500 if you were alone and ₹250 if you had a girl with you. Occasionally Simlai would let us in for free, but that was rare.

This was one of the few times in my life that I felt maybe I didn't have enough. One Sunday morning, my father noticed that I was looking upset and asked me what was wrong. I told him about how we would all go out and when we went to the Park, everyone would go into Someplace Else and I'd make some excuse and stay out in the lobby. I said that it was mostly okay, but just once in a while, I'd like to be able to go in as well. He asked me what I needed and I said that if I could get pocket money of two thousand rupees a month, I'd be able to live like a king. My father started giving me two thousand rupees from that month on, but I still could never get myself to pay to get into Someplace Else.

Our other watering hole was CCFC—The Calcutta Cricket and Football Club. The challenge with getting a drink there was that all the waiters had seen us grow up in front of them. If we asked for a beer or an alcoholic drink, the waiter would threaten to tell our parents. More often than not, that was enough to get us to order a cola. At least in the early days. Eventually, as our parents began to accept that their kids were of legal drinking age, we did just fine. I was fortunate to have wonderful parents in this regard (and every other regard). I remember receiving a phone call at home one evening from a friend who asked me what I was doing. I said I was having a drink. He asked if my parents were out. I said, 'No, I'm drinking with them!' I'm quite sure he fell off his chair. Such things were unheard of in those days.

Last orders at the CCFC were at 11 p.m. and the bar would close at midnight. As soon as the bell for last orders was rung, you could see frenzied action all around. A table with six people would suddenly order twelve whiskeys, eight vodkas, eight rums and six beers. Every inch of the table would be covered with glasses containing alcohol, and the binge would go on from 11 p.m. till 12 a.m. It would be 12.30 a.m. by the time the staff managed to herd everyone out.

One of the legendary figures at the club was an elderly gentleman by the name of Biraj da. Biraj da was in his sixties and the only man in the world I knew who regularly went out drinking with his wife, his mother-in-law and his girlfriend! I still remember how he introduced us to them—'This is my wife, this is my lovely mother-in-law, and this is my hehehehehe!'

Biraj da was a big drinker and an insanely good darts player. He'd be unable to stand straight, but if you picked a number on the dart board, he would sway close to the board, release the dart, and hit your number. Every single time. I remember a wonderful tale he told us about going home drunk one night and wanting to go to the bathroom. This was the exchange with his wife that he narrated to us.

Biraj da: My darling, please take me to the bathroom.

Wife: You are a bloody drunkard. You go yourself. I'm not taking you.

Ten minutes later:

Biraj da: My lovely wife. Please come and see this amazing phenomenon. I go to the bathroom. I open the door. Light come on. I close the door. Light go off. Automatically.

Wife: What?

He takes her to the location and carries on speaking.

Biraj da: See! I open the door. Light come on. I close the door. Light go off. Amazing.

Wife: You bastard. You've pissed in the refrigerator!

A lot of the fun we had was at night, after the club closed. A new bridge had opened up called the Vidyasagar Setu and it was a done thing to go for a drive across the bridge at night. It was Calcutta's Golden Gate Bridge and when lit up, it looked absolutely stunning. On days when the famous Victoria Memorial was lit up as well, the views from the bridge were gorgeous. Also, just after the bridge, where you had to turn around to come back, there was a roundabout where the car's tyres would make a screeching sound—think *Fast and Furious: Tokyo Drift*. For nineteen-year-olds, that was about as exciting as it could get.

Of course, if we wanted to add a level of excitement, all we had to do was sit in my friend Amit's car. Amit wore ridiculously high-power glasses, and with the dim lighting, he could barely see the road. So the guy sitting in the passenger seat would have to tell him when and how much to turn. Before you think it, yes, even I'm surprised that a stupid lot like us survived to tell these tales.

The other kind of mischief we got up to was comparatively innocent. We'd stop a taxi and ask the driver if he'd like to go to the airport. If he said yes, we'd tell him to go, and then run away. Sometimes we'd step into a crowd in the evening and a few of us would randomly point at the sky and exclaim, 'Oh my God. Look at that.' Before you knew it, a dozen people would be looking at the sky in the same direction and we would have left the scene.

We once stumbled upon a hawker of undergarments advertising his wares in a crowded market. The brand name was Gopal. He was shouting, 'Gopal *ka ganji pehno*. Gopal *ka underwear pehno*.' (Wear Gopal's vest. Wear Gopal's underwear.) How could we resist telling him, '*Agar hum* Gopal *ka underwear pehnenge*, Gopal *kya pehnega?*' (If we wear Gopal's underwear, then what will he wear?)

One of my closest friends at this point, Ketan, had just started dating a girl. I remember, one night, we were all at a party for the La' Martiniere School Founders' Day celebration. He decided to sneak out with his woman. My friend Gaurav and I decided that we would follow him with our lights off. He went home to drop her and parked his car in the dark lane just outside her house. We waited for three minutes to give the young man a head start and then suddenly drove up behind his car with lights flashing, horn sounding and tires screeching. I'm quite confident his lady love's curses that night were enough to set us on the path to hell.

That dark lane is the repository of another story as well. Sometimes we'd drive along shouting out the names of the residents of the building we were going past—Vandana Apartment in Alipore, if you need to know. Once Chetan, Ketan and I were driving past and just to tease Ketan, we decided to call out his girlfriend's father's name. Just as we did, the car passed the lane and we saw the man himself standing there saying goodbye to some guests. He had obviously heard his name and turned to look. We saw him and immediately ducked, so all he saw was a car going past with no passengers and no driver. Ketan was upset, but we convinced him that it would be okay since he hadn't seen any of us. His girlfriend later gave him the firing of his life because, of course, his car had been recognised!

This was also around the time that I met N. On 9 February 1997, my friend Ritika had a party at her house in Alipore. As I stood on the terrace, having a drink with KD, the door opened and an angel walked in. She wore a grey dress with black stripes and a black sweater was slung over her shoulders. She wore a light lipstick and her kajal highlighted the most beautiful eyes I had ever seen. Eyes that radiated joy.

The attraction only became stronger when we spoke. Intelligent, kind, and all sorts of adorable. I could not imagine that a nicer person existed on our planet, or any others. When I was told there was a boy in her life, I made it my life's mission to present what I had to offer as a suitable alternative. On 20 March, she succumbed to my persuasion and we started dating.

N was a wonderful girl. I was deeply in love with her and quite the romantic. In fact, I'd argue that the late 90s themselves were a time of romance. The smallest thing you could do for a girl was to give her flowers and chocolates. If you had the brains, you'd write her a poem. If you didn't, you'd go to a card shop, copy one down and give it to her. But by far the most romantic thing you could do was to give her a mixed tape. A compilation tape. You see, millennials, in our generation, we had something called an audio cassette. It was used for storing and playing music. And giving a girl

The day I met N

a mixed tape was the greatest show of commitment. It's not like now, when you can drag three files into a device and give it to her. You had to find out all the songs that she loved. Then you had to call all your friends to find out which of them had audiotapes with those songs. Calling your friends wasn't easy either, because we didn't have mobile phones. We had dial-up phones. And if you came from a middle-class family like I did, your mother put a LOCK on the phone. Not a passcode, a physical fucking padlock!

So, you had to wait until you went to play with your friends to ask them for the songs…but when you asked them for those songs, you lost your self-respect. Imagine a macho eighteen-year-old guy going to his friends and saying, 'Hey bro, do you have "Nothing's going to change my love for you"?' How they laughed! The irony was that each of them had that song. They just couldn't admit to it.

But at least we had songs that allowed us to express our love. 'Nothing's going to change my love for you', 'You are the wind beneath my wings', 'Words are all I have'. What the fuck do they have nowadays? I heard a song the other day, by Eminem. These were the words: 'I ain't never seen an ass like that, the way you shake it makes my pee pee go dawing dawing dawing'. WHAT! If my dad EVER gave my mother a song that said, 'I ain't never seen an ass like that', she would smack him so hard his pee pee would never go dawing dawing dawing.

Anyway, we had to find all the songs that the object of our affection loved. We had to get hold of fifteen different tapes that had those songs. We had to time every single song. If your romance was like today's generation's, you would get her a 60-minute tape. Of course I got my girlfriend a 90-minute tape. Because, in our generation, size did matter!

We had to time the songs and make sure the tape played for exactly forty-five minutes on each side, for a gap in the music would have been a gap in commitment. If you had a tape recorder whose rewind button didn't work, you had to turn the tape around, fast forward it, turn it around, and hope as hell that you were in the right place. If you had a tape recorder like I did, whose rewind and fast forward buttons didn't work, what would you do? If you're a thirty-plus reader I know you're shouting the answer out in your head. For those younger than that: In our generation we had something called a pencil. It was used for an activity we called 'writing'. We would take that pencil, stick it in the tape, twirl it around, and feel like fucking ninjas! (For the millennials, twirling the tape with a pencil would manually rewind the tape).

There were many advantages to giving a girl a mixed tape. Like I said, making them wasn't easy. We had these players called two-in-ones. On one side, you'd put the tape which had the song. On the other side, you'd put the blank tape on which you wanted the song recorded. One side had a play button and the other had a play and pause button. You had to press them both with military precision. You had to make little marks on the tape with a pencil after every song. You had to write the name of the song in tiny yet legible handwriting between two lines that were half a centimetre tall and two inches wide. The upside of it all—when you gave a girl a mixed tape, she knew. That you knew how to use your fingers in a coordinated fashion.

Without trying to make this a 'my generation was cooler than your generation' thing, I must add that in my time, when we went out, we went out to have a good time. Nowadays it seems like people go out to take photographs of themselves looking like they are having a good time. They could be at the most boring party ever, but five guys will get together, take a photograph, stick it up on Facebook and say, Oh my god…last night was EPIC! Sorry, I meant—OMG last night was EPIC!

I don't even understand the use of the word 'epic'. The Ramayan was an epic. The Illiad was an epic. You going out, getting drunk and passing out in a pool of your own piss is not epic. Also, I do not understand the concept of a selfie. As far as I am concerned, a selfie is photographic masturbation. This feels so much like a hashtag generation. In our time, there were no tags. Just hash.

All I'm saying is, we grew up in a simpler time. I used to wash my head with soap. If your parents were rich, maybe you used shampoo. But we just considered that liquid soap. In fact, when liquid soap first came to India in the form of a hand wash, nobody actually believed that it could do a proper job of cleaning. So yeah, you used shampoo if you were a rich kid. But conditioners—nobody even knew what that was. I remember the first time I saw conditioner. There was some foreign kid in the shower cubicle next to mine in school. He said, 'Bro, you should try this hair product. It's a conditioner.' Now, I looked at what was inside that bottle. In fact, every man, the first time he sees conditioner, isn't thinking it's conditioner. I'll be honest, I had to admire the kid for wanting to play such a prank on me, because that bottle was bloody big. It would have taken him one month to fill it up. So, I did what every guy would do in that situation. I said, 'Bro, you use it first.' And he did. So, I tried it and my hair felt amazing. The next day, I went to a girl in my class and said to her, 'Touch my hair. Doesn't it feel amazing?' She touched it and said it was nicer than that of most boys. I told her, 'I used this amazing hair product. It's called conditioner.' She said, 'I use it all the time.' I said, 'Cool. I'll present you a bottle. In a month.'

Delhi and Calcutta were polar opposites in so many ways. While Delhi was considered a big, bad metropolis with aggressive hot-tempered people and all sorts of potentially dangerous influences, thanks to the hostel I stayed in, I quickly became an insider in this world. Our hostel had kids from similar backgrounds thrown together in a little cocoon and that became the eco-system that we drew from.

In Calcutta, on the other hand, while it was a city I supposedly grew up in, I was an outsider. I had only been there for four months in a year, all the previous nine years. Most of my friends were Chetan's friends and like Mary's little lamb, everywhere that he went, I was sure to go. The only exception to this was KD. KD was the cool guy who played a lot of sport, knew everyone at all the clubs, and all the girls thought he was cute. While I wasn't in the same league as KD in sport or popularity, our friendship was solid and having come from the same boarding school, we became each other's wingmen. We also played a lot of sport together and were fit enough to play a round of golf, followed by fourteen games of squash, before going for a swim. When Chetan joined us on the golf course, we gambled. High stakes. A packet of Chicklets chewing gum that cost two rupees. When our pocket money was increased, the stakes evolved to a cola that cost five rupees and then eventually to lunch, which at the club might cost the princely sum of fifty rupees.

Left to right: KD, me, Chetan, Gaurav and Micky, Valentine's Day 1997

These years were an interesting time in my life and very different to the years gone by. In school my focus had always been on trying to 'win' and achieve as many accolades as I could in every field. In my college years, bereft of any form of achievement, my focus shifted to relationships. To friendships. My sense of self came from them. Or maybe I shouldn't say sense of self. My sense of anything, really. They were the crutch that held me up. I had only a few close friends and was never part of a group or clique. Even when there were opportunities to meet new people through rounds of golf, for example, I chose not to go. My dad wasn't the most social person on the planet and, given a choice, I preferred to play that round of golf with him. He was my best friend and he still is.

Those were years when I may have had some fun, but I was on very shaky ground. As a comedian, my instinct is to go for the laugh, so I've spent this chapter relating fun incidents without delving deeper. I had one foot in Delhi and one foot in Calcutta, and if you lived in Allahabad and looked up, you'd have got a terrible view! See, I've done it again. Professional hazard.

The fact is that the superstar from school had had his moment of glory taken away from him, his foundational belief system of all-round development had been thrown into a dustbin, and he felt deprived of an experience he had looked forward to all his life—college. His self-esteem was slowly eroding and he was beginning to lose the confidence to succeed at anything. The future looked anything but bright. Everything seemed to be going downhill.

one step at a time

One of the biggest challenges young people in India face is that of competition. Being a country of over 1.3 billion with the largest 'young' population in the world means that there are always a large number of people fighting over a small number of things. Or, even if there are a large number of things available, there are an exponentially larger number of people who want the same things. A lot of young people who go abroad to study for an undergraduate degree do so because they have the money but can't get into colleges of their choice in India. It's easier to get into Harvard than into a nursery school in Delhi. Almost!

Job-hunting after just an undergraduate degree, that too a bachelor's in commerce, isn't an easy task. A waiter in a five-star hotel has that level of qualification at the very least. Therefore, alongside my undergraduate qualification, I started other courses of study to make myself more attractive to potential employers. In addition to the postgraduate diploma in sales and marketing that I completed from the National Institute of Sales, I also started studying for the Foundation Examination of the Institute of Chartered Accountants of India. In November 1996, I gave the exam and, much to my surprise, was ranked forty-fifth across India in a field of over 100,000 examinees. What made this achievement even more remarkable by my standards was that two weeks before writing the exams, I had been 'evicted' from my home.

We lived in a flat rented by my father's company. The landlord wanted the flat back before the lease expired. In October 1996, while my parents were on holiday abroad, I was sitting at the dining table and studying with my friend Gaurav. At midday, the doorbell rang, I opened the door, and before I knew it, thirty goons had pushed their way into the flat. They walked in and physically restrained both Gaurav and me and immediately cut the phone lines. They then started dismantling everything in the flat and throwing things out. Furniture, clothes, artefacts, food, kitchen utensils...EVERYTHING. It took five or six hours, but by the end of it, everything we owned was out on the street with a chunk of stuff getting stolen along the way. I remember feeling grateful that my mother was not in town because she would have had a breakdown.

By 4 p.m., the news had spread and some of my friends showed up to help. They tried calling the police, but the cops had been bribed and did not heed the call. My dad had only recently been able to save enough money for us to buy a flat of our own and luckily I had the keys to that. So we set about arranging trucks to transport all our stuff. By the time we managed to get the last object into the new house, it was exactly midnight. It had been a long and traumatic day. The only people for whom the trauma was greater were firstly my parents, who felt bad about not being around—I was only nineteen, after all. And secondly, my friend Ketan's girlfriend because when those goons broke in, she was in my bedroom making out with him!

Once you clear the CA Foundation Examination, you are expected to study and appear for the Intermediate examinations and after that the Finals. Studying for the Intermediate involved giving practice tests early on Sunday mornings. After looking at the details of the course and realising exactly how dull and insipid it was, I had a chat with my father. I told him that they were teaching an outdated course with twenty-year-old material that had no relevance in this day and age and I did not want to continue with it. While the outdated content was a major reason for my reluctance, an equally major reason was that I could not bear to wake up early in the morning. Clearly, I had my priorities right. A lucrative career was nowhere near as high on my list as having a lie-in on Sunday! Like my mother, I am just not a morning person. I will go to vast lengths to avoid anything that requires me to set an alarm in the morning. The only exceptions being golf, a motorcycle ride, and sex. In that order.

We decided that I should consider doing a master's in business administration. An MBA. Since I hadn't had the experience of going to a proper college for my undergraduate degree and was altogether disillusioned with higher education in India, we decided that I would give the GMAT and apply to colleges abroad. As I started doing my research, I learnt that I'd need to secure a first division in my undergraduation to get admission into any decent business school. Having almost failed my second year of college, this would be near impossible without reappearing in at least half of the papers from the second year, along with all seven honours papers of my third and final year. That's when I really put my head down and started studying. Not just hard, but smart as well. Earlier, I had tried to study everything, mocking those who focussed on studying the past ten years' question papers and only those questions that had a higher probability of turning up in the exams. This year, I did the opposite. I focussed on the tricks of the trade instead of the trade itself. My strategy worked. My second-year average went up from forty per cent to fifty-five per cent and when combined with the first and third year results, gave me a first class or first division.

For my GMAT I studied a sum total of ten days. I had attended an education fair organised by the British Council, at which I met the head of admissions of the University of Swansea. He said I didn't have enough experience to get admission to his university. I asked him what would happen if I got 700 (out of 800) on the GMAT. He gave me his business card and said that if that happened, I should drop him a line. Realising the importance of the test, I locked myself into a room and during those ten days showed up only for meals, if that.

I gave the GMAT in a tiny room in Calcutta with three other students and four air conditioners. After freezing my way through the first half, the verbal section, I asked the attendant to turn the temperature up a little. I then answered the mathematics and analytical reasoning sections. Three hours later, my result appeared on the screen. I went home and apologised to my mother. I told her how disappointed I was. I told her I wanted to tell dad in person.

I then went to his office. She had forewarned him. When I reached his cabin, he was at his empathetic best. He said, 'Don't worry, son.' To which I responded, 'Worry about what? I've just got a 710!'

A 700+ on the GMAT was the holy grail and I had knocked it out of the park. It was as good as I could have hoped for. I was in the ninety-ninth percentile, putting me in the top one per cent of the examinees. The first part of the hard work was done. Now I had two more hard bits to tackle—get admission into a good university and get a scholarship.

I decided that I would apply to a few select universities in the US and two or three of the top schools in the UK as well. In those days, a lot of the business schools had similar application essays. With questions like 'Where do you see yourself five years from now' and 'Why do you want to apply to Stanford Business School'. In my infinite wisdom I decided it would be more efficient to copy-paste my answers and therefore sent an application to Harvard Business School telling them why I really wanted to go to Stanford. I knew I would be rejected the second I posted the application and Harvard didn't even bother to send me a rejection letter.

I applied to two schools in the UK. London Business School, which was ranked number one in the UK, required work experience that I did not have. So the two schools I ended up applying to were Manchester Business School, because it was ranked second in the UK, and the University of Oxford because it was the University of Oxford! Manchester gave me admission into their eighteen-month

MBA programme while Oxford, a newer business school, gave me a deferred admission. They asked me to first get two years of work experience. Although Manchester was better known at the time, I figured one couldn't possibly go wrong by betting on Oxford. It might be a new school, but you could go into an igloo in Antarctica and the sole living being in a 700-mile radius would have heard its name. So I decided to roll the dice.

I called the business school at Oxford and told them that while they were my first choice, I wasn't willing to wait two years. If they were to give me admission immediately, I would choose them over the higher ranked schools I had got into. Three hours later I received an email stating that 'the admissions committee had met and decided to give me admission onto the MBA programme in the upcoming academic year'. I was about to become the youngest MBA at Oxford!

All that was left for me to do before leaving was to tick off the small matter of funding. A meagre sum of £30,000 was what the one year would cost me. To put it in perspective, had my father worked nonstop at his starting salary and saved one hundred per cent of it, he would have been able to pay for the cost of my education and living expenses at Oxford...after working for 250 years.

I sat for days on end at the British Council, did my research, and applied for every single scholarship that I could possibly be eligible for. The big one that I was shortlisted for was the Radhakrishnan Scholarship, for which I had to go to Delhi for the interview. I was both nervous and excited because it was a full scholarship. I still remember walking into that room to be interviewed by a panel of five people. They grilled me on why I had left a reputed institution like Hindu College to do a correspondence course. I told them that after nine years in a boarding school I wanted to spend more time with my family and that I also wanted to study a course of my choice. Somehow, the panel, which I now realise was quite elitist, could not fathom how someone from a reputed boarding school could let go of a brand like Hindu College just to prioritise his interests and his family.

I don't know whether it was the fact that I was nervous or unwell, but I felt dizzy during the interview, like I was about to faint. I didn't have the confidence to tell them I was feeling ill, so I gave short answers, said thank you, and left the room. I didn't get the scholarship of course, because how could one possibly confer a prestigious scholarship on a student who had spurned a prestigious college. Either that or there were better candidates than me. I like to tell myself it was the former!

I was, however, able to secure two scholarships, which helped me with half the amount I needed. One of them was from my college at Oxford (Templeton). For the second half, I took a personal loan. Then I wrote to the admissions committee at Oxford and accepted their offer. I also wrote to the admissions guy at the University of Swansea and told him I had got 700+ on my GMAT and was going to Oxford, so thanks but no thanks. Yes, I was still a cocky little shit! And yes, while I am now on Oxford's list of notable alumni in the Wikipedia entry of the business school, they don't exactly put me in the brochure. They're not going around telling people to come spend thousands of pounds on an Oxford MBA so they can become stand-up comedians one day!

Proud parents of the Oxford graduate

With my future somewhat secure, I had a year to kill. I wanted to get some work experience before the MBA and so I got a job with Coca-Cola as a field sales representative. My job required me to walk the streets of Calcutta, shop to shop, trying to convince shopkeepers to stock Coca-Cola.

At this time I also applied to the Himalayan Mountaineering Institute (HMI) in Darjeeling for their basic mountaineering course. This twenty-eight-day course gets you to a skill level that sets you up for climbing Mount Everest. Most of the trainees were from the Indian Army. They were trained at HMI and then sent to the glaciers in

Kashmir. There were also three or four civilian idiots like me, who thought we might have what it took.

The first week of the course was spent in Darjeeling, learning rock climbing, mountaineering and rescue techniques. Our instructors were very experienced and the field director was a man called Nwang Gombu—the first man to scale Mount Everest twice. There was a strenuous training session in the morning that was run by an ex-army commando. At the end of the workout, you were required to pick up a man your weight and run up half a hill with him. Then he carried you and ran up the forty-five degree ascent. Believe me when I say you'd rather be carrying than be carried because the way you are carried has your testicles bouncing off the carrier's shoulder with every step—very painful indeed.

With other trainees at Chaurikhang base camp,
14,000 feet above sea level

Before the trek to base camp, a fitness test was administered and those who passed were taken to the glacier at 16,000 feet to learn mountaineering techniques. At the end of ten days of training on ice, we summited two peaks. Rinnoch at 17,000 feet was technically challenging while B.C. Roy peak at 18,000 feet tested our skills on snow and ice.

At the end of the course, I calculated that I had bathed four times in that entire month! Brushing one's teeth was hard enough because every morning we had to break through six inches of snow inside a barrel to get to some water and within three seconds of it coming into contact with our skin, we'd be freezing.

My father had done this same course exactly thirty years before me. In his time there were heavy rains and landslides, and rescue missions had to be sent for them.

The course had an award for the best cadet. I was the fittest trainee, an excellent rock climber, and very good with my mountaineering techniques. The award practically had my name written on it. However, one day, one of the trainees lost his watch and our instructors asked us to open our backpacks to see if any of us had stolen it. I objected. Just because someone had misplaced something, how could suspicion be cast on every member of the group? The lead instructor decided that this was a good enough reason to take the best cadet award away from me. It was the army way: questioning the orders of a 'superior' was out of the question. I felt terrible because once again it felt like something I rightfully deserved had been taken away from me. In school it was because I wouldn't open my mouth and this time it was because I wouldn't keep it shut!

Doing the mountaineering course had required me to let go of my job with Coca-Cola. After the course I joined Unilever, which at the time was called Hindustan Lever Limited in India. Once again, it was a sales job and I continued to walk the streets of Calcutta, this time trying to persuade shopkeepers to stock ice cream instead of cola.

In September 1999 I went to Oxford to join the MBA programme. This was my golden ticket. One that I believed would finally equip me to get back on a path of achievement and success. A path that I had deviated from after school.

At Oxford, the course of study is conducted by the university but students live in 'colleges'. My MBA batch was spread across forty different colleges, where they lived with students from different disciplines. It made for a very enriching experience. My college was Templeton, and it was only for management students, and slightly out of town. It wasn't an ideal location; the best place to be was in the city centre where most of the colleges were. Also, since I wasn't living with students from other disciplines, it felt like I wasn't quite getting the full Oxford experience. However, Templeton was giving me a £5000 scholarship and that was that.

It was a rough year for me. On a one-year MBA programme they give you more work than is humanly possible to do. Therefore, the three skills you are forced to develop very quickly are time management, prioritisation, and the ability to handle pressure. Our class had students from twenty-seven different countries, ages ranging from twenty-two (that was me) to Robert at fifty-three—he was older than even my father. I can put my hand over my heart and say that I learnt far more from my fellow students that year than I did from any teacher. We worked in groups and under pressure and just observing how sharp minds across a range of age groups, backgrounds and countries functioned was truly eye opening. In fact, on the rare occasion, I even ended up leading a project and assigning team roles because the other, more strong-minded members did not get along with each other.

It wasn't the work pressure that troubled me at Oxford. It was the financial pressure. The thought of not getting a job in the UK was scary. It would mean returning to India and having to pay back my loans over god knows how many decades. I remember, that entire year, I looked at Starbucks only from the outside. I never had the guts to actually walk in because I could not imagine how anyone could pay two pounds for a cup of coffee. I'm not joking when I say I wrote up more job applications than probably my entire MBA class put together. Every time I got a rejection letter from a company, I would reapply to them. Sometimes their admin would change and I would get called for an interview the second time around, LEK Consulting being an example. Others like Bain and Co. wrote saying thank you for reapplying to us but we still don't want you! The rejection letters had a standard format—thank you for applying, we had a highly skilled applicant pool, really liked reading your application, but no thanks and good luck for the future. We called these PFO letters—please fuck off!

Getting a job was even tougher for me because of the work permit issue. If you were not a European Union citizen, the company hiring you had to show that no EU citizen was qualified to do the job they were hiring a non-EU citizen for. Which meant not only proof of advertising the job and interviewing potential candidates from European countries, but also showing your unique credentials for it. This was hard enough to do for experienced professionals with a specialised skill set, but a 23-year-old who had walked the streets of Calcutta selling Coca-Cola?

The University Careers Service told me that if they really liked you, they would make the effort. However, I never put my nationality on my CV because that could have been an immediate cause for rejection. I figured I'd let potential employers invest time and effort interviewing me, and if they liked me and wanted to employ me, then I'd tell them that I'd need a work permit. Hopefully they'd make the effort because it might be easier than going through the interview process with another candidate all over again.

I can't even remember the number of firms I interviewed with. I was an anomaly for recruiters because I was at an undergraduate age and with almost no work experience but with a postgraduate qualification. That made it difficult for them to place me. At a consulting firm, I would be too qualified to be an analyst, yet not qualified enough to be a consultant.

My first ever interview was in December 1999, two months after starting the MBA programme. It was with the Investment Banking Division of Goldman Sachs, the most coveted job at any business school. I still remember one of the questions they asked—'If we gave you £1000 to invest, how would you invest it?' I promptly replied, 'I'd give it to my father. He invests the money for our family.'

Understandably, I was politely asked to get out. I was only disappointed they didn't ask my dad to come and interview!

Another interview I attended was for a marketing position at L'Oreal at their offices at Hammersmith in London. London was a one-hour train journey away from Oxford, ninety minutes if you took the bus. My interviewer was quite possibly the most attractive woman I had met in my life. A voluptuous blonde in a tight red dress. I remember telling myself, CJ, focus on the questions, not on her. I received their rejection letter in my email inbox before my train pulled into Oxford station. Raging hormones: 1; CJ: 0.

College life at Templeton was fun, though. I made some wonderful friends among both students and staff. I was on the college squash team. Since we were a small college, our cooks, Tim and Andy, were on the team as well. As the college also did executive education, there were a lot of fancy dinners for the executives when they were on programmes. Occasionally we riffraff had high-table dinners too. Since we knew Tim and Andy, after these dinners were over, every bottle of wine or port that had been opened and was unfinished would find its way to the common room. If we were lucky, some cheese as well. Many a drunken night was spent toasting the knights of the Templeton kitchen!

We weren't always well behaved on those drunken nights. The occasional fire alarm was set off so we could figure out who was sleeping with whom in college. One day, we found an old, unused piano lying in our common room. Four individuals who shall remain unnamed decided to take it out into the garden and, one sledgehammer swing at a time,

At the Templeton College boathouse with MBA classmates and Jehan

reduce it to pieces. We didn't think much of it afterwards, until we learned that the piano was on rent!

On the rare occasion that we paid for drinks ourselves, we would frequent a place called Maxwells. They did student deals on pitchers of alcohol and they did a mean Long Island Iced Tea. In case you're not familiar with the cocktail, it contains all the whites—vodka, gin, light rum and tequila. It also contains triple sec and cola. And regret. It's an incredibly potent concoction. If you go to a bartender and say, 'Hey buddy, fuck me up', he will serve you an LIT. Almost every single time we went there, someone had to be carried out.

There was just one time I remember (or don't remember) getting particularly drunk at Oxford. At the end of the second term, we were supposed to give exams for the courses we'd completed in our first and second terms. It was an insane workload. I slept for four hours in seventy-two. After the exams, we went to Café Boheme, a bar close to New College (it's called New College because it's new—it came into being in 1379) and I drank £40 worth of Vodka Red Bull. I woke up twenty-four hours later in the common room of my college with no memory of how I got there.

New College, incidentally, is where I was seated next to a Harvard professor at dinner once. He was due to give a speech at Oxford the next day. I casually told him this popular Oxford story over dinner, which to my surprise he opened his speech with the following day: A professor from Harvard came to visit Oxford and as he walked through Christchurch College, he noticed how immaculate the grass was. He walked over to the groundskeeper and said, 'I come from Harvard. The best university in the world. And yet, we don't have grass as nice as yours. How do you do it?' To which the groundskeeper replied, 'It's very simple, sir. You get good seed. You get good manure. You water it. And then you roll the grass for EIGHT HUNDRED YEARS.'

At Oxford, once again, I was an outsider. Unlike New College, which was in the centre of town, the location of my college put me at a physical distance from all the action. The fact that I was much younger and a lot more inexperienced than practically every student in my class meant that I was constantly unsure whether my point of view was worthy enough to be put forward in a discussion. And the financial background that I came from meant that I could not even consider participating in the many different activities of my classmates because I just didn't have the change to spare. In this aspect, my good friend, squash partner and college mate Jehan stood on common ground with me. So we'd hang out together a lot and eat whatever we could within our budget. Oxford colleges have eighty balls in each of the three ten-week terms. Jehan and I attended just one. It was the one that we got discounted tickets for and which didn't require us to rent a black gown. We went in the only suits that we possessed.

Jehan and I with Sue Dopson, Dean at Templeton College

A few days before our second term exams, IBM came to campus to recruit for their consulting practice. Although I had far too much work on my plate, jobs were always a priority, so on principle I went for the first-round campus interview. To my surprise, they shortlisted me. The second round was at an Assessment Centre. Which meant you would go to an external location for two days. At the end of day one, they'd give you work that would keep you up all night and test you on it the next day. It was far too close to the date of my exams, but there was no way I wasn't going to go. So I did.

Unlike most of the other firms I had interviewed with, these guys were warmer, friendlier, and if I may say so, a homelier bunch. Soon after the Assessment Centre task was done, I was informed that I had made the cut for the final-round interviews. The final round would be with Paul Clutterbuck, the head of the financial services consulting practice. Since it was a final-round interview, I treated myself to the train to London instead of the bus. I had two vodka shots on the way there and prayed he wouldn't be a voluptuous man in a tight red dress. I reached the offices of IBM in Southbank on the banks of the River Thames. I had prepared answers for all the questions I thought I'd get, but I wasn't prepared for what the charismatic Paul Clutterbuck threw at me midway through the interview. 'You've got the job,' he said. 'How much money do you want?' Sorry, WHAT? I thought I'd heard wrong. Weren't they supposed to send you an email later? Or give you a call? Or send you a letter saying they really liked you but couldn't give you the job?

I wasn't prepared for this. So I simply said, 'Whatever you think is fair, Paul. Fair market rate for my skills and experience.' As it happened, the position I was being interviewed for was associate consultant. It was placed above analyst and below consultant. A week later, I received an offer from IBM with a salary higher than I expected. Immediately after that, I got a call from the recruitment department saying there had been a mistake and the package I should have been offered was £10,000 less. I told them this was what Paul had said I'd get. Recruitment decided we'd meet midway and I started off on a salary £5000 higher than I had expected. Thank. You. Paul.

Paul and I have stayed in touch after he retired from IBM. In 2016, I met him in Miami for lunch. I asked him if he remembered why he had decided to hire me, and these were his exact words: 'Of course. You had the right academic background, but that wasn't it. I could see that you had the right personality that would fit in with everyone else. It wasn't teamwork, it was the human chemistry that was most important to me. You had it, and by the looks of it, you obviously still do. When the chips are down, humans need to know how to behave with each other.'

With my first super boss, Paul Clutterbuck, in Miami

There are inflexion points in every person's life. And while some say that you make your own fate, I will always be grateful to Paul. His nod changed my life forever.

On 6 December 2000, at 9 a.m. sharp, a twenty-three-year-old associate consultant reported to the offices of IBM Consulting UK at 76 Upper Ground, South Bank, London. He wore a dark suit, a crisply ironed white shirt, and shiny black shoes. He was nervous and excited. This was the beginning of the middle-class dream. He had landed a job with a multinational firm in London and he was going to work his ass off and steadily climb his way to the top. And then some.

He was escorted to his staff manager Tony Roper, who informed him that he would soon meet the line manager he would be reporting to—Alan Greenwood. Alan was a kind, bespectacled and somewhat eccentric man who offered the following words of advice to me on my first day. He said, 'It's important for you to stand tall but just a little taller than the others.' By which I inferred that you had to stand just a little taller to get noticed, but if anyone tried to stand much taller than the others, somebody would cut them down. I've learned since then that this piece of advice applies in almost any industry in the world, comedy included.

Alan told me that I needed to go for two weeks of consulting training. I'd have to apply for each of the weeks separately and the IBM training centres that conducted the courses were in Belgium and Palisades, in upstate New York. Obviously I applied to New York. Given that the training would be for five working days, I could get two back-to-back weeks in the US and spend the free weekend in the middle in Manhattan. Another new recruit from Denmark, a tall, good-looking young man called Morten Schlosser also applied for it and lo and behold, we both got accepted to the New York programmes.

Morten and I concocted a plan. Since we had the weekend free between the first and second week of training, we would share a hotel room that weekend. That way, we could bill it to the company in one person's name and then get another room in Manhattan after the second week of training, which we could bill in the second person's name. That would give us an additional weekend in Manhattan. On the last night of the second weekend, he and I went out in separate directions. We had packed our bags in advance because we anticipated a late night and we had a 7 a.m. flight back to London.

I had a crazy night. I hadn't slept the night before because I had been at an all-night party from which I returned at 8 a.m. And that same evening, I went out, drank a bottle of vodka, neat, came back to our hotel room, threw up in the bathroom and passed out. I passed out in a hotel room in Manhattan in New York and woke up the following evening when our plane touched down at Heathrow in London. I don't know what drunken stories you might have, but getting plastered and waking up on a different continent is pretty out there. (I had to force myself to not use the word 'epic'!)

Morten had carried me to the airport, checked me in, put me on the plane and made me lie down across four empty seats in Economy. And as a reward for his efforts, he put an open *Playboy* magazine on my chest. No wonder the cabin crew didn't disturb me during the flight.

IBM turned out to be a mixed blessing for me. On the upside, I lived frugally and even though I had a very low salary relative to my MBA classmates, over the next four years I paid back all my loans. I owned five office shirts that I would wear from Monday to Friday, wash on Saturday and iron on Sunday. On the downside, the corporate exhaust pipe pissed all over my dreams of learning and growth, and any career ambitions that I had. 2001–2004 was a difficult time to be in a job. The dot-com bust had happened in 2000. Projects were few and far between, and if you didn't have industry experience, there was no way you'd be placed on one.

As a junior at a consulting firm, you are dependent on principal consultants getting you projects. I didn't know any principal consultants. My manager suggested that I learn to network. I figured sport was the only thing I might have in common with guys much senior to me. I was a member of the Oxford and Cambridge Club, so I invited a principal consultant, Jon Brock, known to be a legend in process consulting, to a game of squash. Three games in, as Jon lunged to reach a drop shot, there was a loud noise. Snap! He had torn his Achilles tendon. He was in a non-walking plaster for the next six weeks and a walking plaster for six more weeks after that. It was my most significant impact on IBM's bottom line that year.

This was a tough time for the UK economy. I didn't know a single person from my entire MBA class, at least in London, who one year after the MBA still had the same job they had started out with. Luckily for me, IBM was a large organisation and because (a) I was good with people and (b) I was a low-cost resource, I was able to move from one department to another while others around me lost their jobs. I held six or seven different jobs over three years. Associate consultant in financial services, associate consultant in the wealth management practice, a role in the communications practice, a business services role working for a man who looked like a 1970s porn star and, finally, a business controls role that was dull as dishwater but at which I excelled. I also helped the recruitment team hire MBAs into the consulting practice, reviewing CVs and conducting early-round interviews.

Eventually, bored out of my skull at the business controls job, I quit the position and applied for an internal role in a research department. I was placed in an office in a town called Basingstoke. On my first day there, I left home at 7 a.m. and reached the office at 8.45 a.m. I'd had to take the underground to Waterloo station, catch a train from there to Basingstoke station and then walk ten minutes to the office. I entered a room that had eight people in it, each of whom looked like they had not met another human being outside that room in ten years. My new boss Bill Harmer came in at 9.30 a.m. I told him I had made a mistake and that I could not possibly work here. He said that meant I would be internally unemployed at a time when there were very few jobs around. I would risk getting axed, lose my work permit and visa and have to go back to India. If I didn't stick around, I could lose my job, he said. I told him, if I did stick around, I'd lose my life.

I don't know if it was a low tolerance for boredom or an appetite for risk that made me take the decision. Or maybe just my hatred of shitty commuting! I knew what it was like to travel for three hours a day on a local bus in Calcutta. The morning journey was still bearable. The evening journey had me standing for ninety minutes on a bumpy ride, stuffed into the vehicle like a sardine among hundred others, holding a handrail above my head while taking in the sweet scents of a hundred armpits holding handrails after a full day's work in humid Calcutta weather. It could make anyone throw up. The thought of having to do this again in a different country was unbearable. But was it worth taking a potentially life-changing risk just because I couldn't bear the work environment and the commute? It could turn out to be a very stupid decision. In the past I had walked out of the glamorous field of chartered accountancy (I trust you recognise sarcasm when you hear it) to find myself walking the humid streets of Calcutta for ten hours a day in order to earn ₹4000 a month. Until I was rescued by the Oxford MBA. Would this gamble send me back to that again? To a hundred armpits in Calcutta because I didn't want to be smelling a hundred armpits in London? I would soon find out.

11 September 2001 had changed the world. The focus on safety and security and the prevention of terror attacks had prompted IBM to set up a Homeland Security division. It was a new incubator. An internal opening was advertised there. It sounded exciting, so I decided to apply. Yes, a brown man, soon after 9/11, applying for a job in UK Homeland Security. I was invited to interview with the head of the safety and security practice for IBM in Europe. I showed up to this interview with my shirt sleeves rolled up and

wearing a sleeveless sweater. During the interview, he asked me about my education. I told him I had an MBA from Oxford and patronisingly started to explain what an MBA was. At this point he mentioned that there was no need for me to explain because he had an MBA as well. I followed this up by asking him where he had got his degree from and when he said Manchester Business School, I responded, 'Ah, never mind then'! I still don't know why I said that at a job interview. I was either a stupid fuck, a cocky fuck or just didn't give a fuck.

The way it worked in the Homeland Security division was that after the interviews, they were obliged to do background checks. Government agencies like MI5 and MI6 had to certify that you were not on the opposite team. Proper James Bond stuff! At the end of the interview, bossman said, 'If you get offered the job, we are going to have to check if we can hire you.' Now, I had been seeing a lot of Ali G at the time. (Ali G was a character played by actor and comedian Sasha Baron Cohen, of a white man pretending to be a black gangster. If you haven't seen it, you must. He's brilliant.) Without a moment's hesitation I replied, as Ali G would have, 'Is it coz I is black?' I don't know whether the boss thought I was qualified for the job or whether this little interaction put him in a spot or had anything to do with it...but I got the damn job!

the 171

Living in London was an adventure. When I first moved, I wanted to ensure that I could give my entire focus to my job. I wanted to ensure that I didn't have much to take care of on the home front. So I found myself accommodation in a place called Vincent House, at Pembridge Square in Notting Hill. Vincent House provided serviced accommodation. I got a tiny single room with a bathroom en suite, a single bed, a small desk, a small cupboard and a tiny balcony. If I were to guess, I'd say my room was about 8x12 feet. The property provided you with bed linen and towels. Someone cleaned the room once every couple of days and, most importantly, they served breakfast and dinner in the dining room downstairs. There was also a common room with a bar and a billiards table. This was to be my home for the first nine months in London.

Notting Hill was a lovely place to live in and, once in a while, I would treat myself to food at a pub on Kensington Church Street—The Churchill Arms. Till date, it is one of my favourite places to eat in London. They have a Thai restaurant at the back of the pub, in a butterfly conservatory. In those days, you could get a full meal for £5. If you ever go, I'd recommend Number 15 on the menu—chicken with cashew nuts and rice. It's delicious. Also, try and go on a summer's day (there are about four days of summer in the entire year in England) so you can enjoy the wonderful flowers they have there.

Nine months into staying in London, I made a few friends and learnt that there were economies of scale when it came to accommodation. Living with one other person, or preferably two people, in a larger flat significantly brought down your rent. A friend of a friend had a room going in a flat in Hammersmith and so I moved in there with two girls. I got on very well with one but not so much with the girl whose house it was. I don't remember what some of the points of contention were, but I was immature enough to get into the shower early and let the hot water run out!

Around this time, I started hanging out a lot with two people. A close friend of mine from business school, Shahin, and another friend from Calcutta, Kabir. We would frequent the Trocadero in Piccadilly Circus where we would regularly go bowling. The lanes were managed by a Nepali man called Shambhu and he'd occasionally give us an extra free game. The three of us decided to get a flat together. We went house-hunting and eventually settled on a beautiful property in Notting Hill. It was a bit of a walk from the nearest underground station, but it had wooden floors and a lovely little garden at the back. It was on the ground floor, and the balcony looked down upon the road where the Notting Hill Carnival took place. We made grand plans of selling stuff to revellers during the carnival and making ourselves a little fortune to recover some of the rent. We all gave notice to our current landlords, went to see the house again on a Wednesday and confirmed that we would move in on Friday morning. My mum was coming from India on Friday afternoon and I thought it would be a wonderful surprise for her.

On Friday morning, the letting agent called me screaming, demanding to know what we had done. I didn't understand. He said the house was flooded, the wooden floors were destroyed, and that it would be three months before the house was inhabitable. What! My mum was coming that afternoon and I was homeless.

I called Kabir and Shahin and appraised them of the situation. We all took the rest of the day off from our various jobs, called a bunch of different letting agents and planned to see as many houses as we could that afternoon. My poor mother landed at Heathrow airport and was brought to a Starbucks in Notting Hill, where she sat with her luggage while three homeless young men went looking for a house. The second or third house I saw was Flat 3, 171 Sussex Gardens. It was a three-bedroom flat with a high ceiling, two bathrooms, of which one was en suite, a large living room and a small kitchen. It was available for £495 per week. I didn't even wait for Kabir and Shahin to see the place. I told the agent we wanted it, I was happy to pay him immediately and move in twenty minutes later. Of course, it doesn't work that way. They needed bank references and the like, so early next week would be the earliest it would happen. I said fine. I called the boys and told them the deal was done. Each of us then called various friends to give us shelter until we could move into our new home, one that as chance would have it, would give us some of the happiest years of our lives. Shahin later confessed to me that when we went to see the Notting Hill flat on Wednesday, he had noticed that one of the bathrooms had a tap near the pot that would allow us to wash our bums. Few things are more exciting for Asians, who aren't brought up using toilet paper. He wanted to ensure that the jewel in the crown (or throne) of our new kingdom was functioning properly. And in testing said jewel, he may inadvertently have left the tap on!

Our flat at Sussex Gardens, 'The 171' as we called it, was a wonderful place to live in. We were a two-minute walk from Hyde Park and Lancaster Gate station on the Central Line of the London Underground. We were also a two-minute walk from Paddington station, which had the Circle and District Lines, the Bakerloo Line, and the Heathrow Express, which took you directly to the airport in fifteen minutes. Paddington station had trolleys for luggage, and we often used these when we had guests—once we figured out that, instead of a £1 coin, you could put in an old Indian five-rupee coin and therefore didn't need to take the trolley back to the station later. We also had a neighbourhood supermarket, a bank, and great places to eat at. Our regular haunt was a hole-in-the-wall pizza place called Fresco. It was a two-minute walk away, was cheap, and had amazing pizzas. They took twenty minutes to deliver, so we would call and order ahead instead, and one of us would go and pick up the pizzas. Deciding who would go was a different story altogether. The job was assigned to the person who lost a forty-five-minute indoor golf tournament! We had bought a little artificial putting green with a hole in it that was placed in the hallway. The play would start in another room and each match was custom designed. Over the coffee table, around the leg of another piece of furniture, in between two cups...the combinations were endless. Any contact with any object or wall was a one-stroke penalty. The person who took the most shots to finish the hole would lose, you'd think, but no. As soon as the hole was lost, an argument would be made for a best of three. And if three different people lost back-to-back, a fourth match would have to be played so that a final loser could be decided.

Shahin, Kabir and I made a good team in the kitchen as well. Shahin cooked the non-veg food and was the best cook of us all. I was responsible for making the rice, daal and raita. Kabir would do the dishes. We also had a favourite place that we called in from—a South Indian restaurant called Kovalam that did fabulous Kerala dishes. Their meat masala dosa and fish curry were to die for! We also soon learnt that the frozen parathas available at a particular grocery store were delicious. Our two eating-out places were in Bayswater—Khan's the regular place and Standard Indian for when we wanted to treat ourselves. You could get a full meal at Khan's for £5 and Standard cost twice as much. Standard had a great mutton keema while Khan's had a good butter chicken. Although, if you used your hands to eat the butter chicken, it took three days to get the artificial colouring off them.

Given our central location in London and the fact that London is at the centre of the world, there were always people passing through. We enjoyed keeping open house, and for most of the year, we had guests. Friends and family from different parts of the world invariably came to stay with us. Our living room had a sofa bed and the guests (depending on their seniority) would normally take one of our bedrooms and we would sleep on the sofa bed. It was always a treat when we had a house guest whose cooking expertise went beyond our limited range.

Left to right: Me, mum, Kabir and Shahin

We had fantastic neighbours as well. Two floors above us lived two lovely Indian men—Sid and Chris. Chris had the most eccentric family and wonderful stories to tell. One of my favourites was of his uncle who lived on a tea plantation and had always wanted to be a pilot. He had built himself a wooden cockpit on the branches of a tree. On the odd day, he would pull on World War II pilot glasses and sit on the tree pretending to fly a plane! Chris was dating a Greek girl called Katerina—their third flatmate. A comedy sketch artist at the time (she now does stand-up), Kats was a bundle of energy and one of the most fun people I've ever met. Sid and I had birthdays a week apart, so we often had joint birthday parties at our place.

Parties at The 171 were the stuff of legend. A hundred people would show up and stay till four in the morning. And we had a house large enough to accommodate them. At the time, Shahin was dating a Colombian girl who was his colleague, and she would make sangria for our parties. This sangria was made in three large bathing buckets, Afterwards, whatever booze was left in the house was poured into them. It was a cocktail deadly enough to severely intoxicate a large dinosaur.

Sid had a fancy for a girl in his office. I forget her first name, but I remember that her surname was Wilson. The story goes that all the girls in his office had songs that had their names in them, except for the attractive Ms Wilson. So Sid had proclaimed very grandly that he would write a song for her. Fast forward a few months to the joint birthday party that Sid and I were throwing at my place. The lovely Ms Wilson decided to grace us with her presence and Sid was plying her with alcohol as best he could. Eventually, a few drinks down, he says to her, 'I've written a song for you. Come up to my flat and I'll play it for you.' Her response could be loosely translated as 'Fuck off, there's no way I'm coming up to your flat. Bring your guitar down if you want.' Sid goes up and returns in ten minutes to explain that it is an electric guitar that is plugged in and cannot be unplugged. After much persuasion, she agrees to go up as long as Chris goes along as well. Chris, being a dutiful wingman, agrees. They go up and Sid proceeds to start playing an old Pink Floyd number...with NO WORDS. This, supposedly, was the song he had written for her with her name in it. Three minutes in, Chris quickly understands that he is faced with two options—to stab himself in the ears or to return to the party. He chooses the latter. We were informed the next day that eventually Ms Wilson and Sid decided to get cosy with each other. One thing led to another and Sid ended up taking his clothes off before attempting to romantically undress Ms Wilson. He first got all her clothes off and then headed for her boots. She was wearing knee-length white boots with long zips that opened them up. He managed to get one boot off and struggled with the zipper of the other, which seemed to be stuck. Seven minutes later, he stood up from the foot of the bed to find his romantic interest fast asleep wearing just one boot. This is why we don't remember her name as she was henceforth referred to as 'One boot Wilson' and my friend Sid never wrote a song for another woman again.

That same night, a young boy whose father worked in the same tea company as my father, came to visit. A wonderful young man, Anurag was planning to study in the UK. I don't know what his past track record of being able to hold a drink was, but his body clearly hadn't done the required training to handle The 171 Sangria. Around midnight, he told me that he was dating this rather attractive girl, Pooja, who we both knew back home. I told him that she was way out of his league and there was no way she would even look at his face. In his wisdom, he decided to call her up in India and put her on the phone with me. Now, here was a woman who has been woken up at 3.30 a.m. by a boyfriend drunk out of his skull at a party on another continent, clearly having a great time. If you've ever been in a relationship, you know this is a recipe for disaster. I don't know what I told Pooja, but it was along the lines of 'I'm really sorry, ma'am. I'd like to apologise for my friend. He's drunk out of his mind. You are the fourth girl he has called who he insists he is dating. I'm sorry for this.' Evil. Pure evil. I know. Anurag spent the next hour on an international call, apologising to Pooja. After the call, he proceeded to get twice as drunk, if that was even possible. It was the night of the Australian Grand Prix. At 4 a.m., six people at various levels of drunkenness were in the living room supposedly watching the race. Anurag woke up and decided that he needed to take a leak. He proceeded to walk towards the dining table and whipped out Little John. My friend Jehan saw this and nudged Shahin, who was sleeping on the couch. Shahin shouted at Anurag, 'Anurag! *Tum wahan pe susu nahi karoge* (don't piss there)! People live here, okay!' Alas, his screams fell on deaf ears. Anurag had let loose on one of the dining chairs.

I don't know what happened after that. I believe Shahin rugby tackled him (from behind and not the front obviously). When we woke up in the morning, Anurag was passed out on the floor with one half of his body in the kitchen and the other half in the hallway. A friend's mother, who was staying with us at the time, had stepped over him to get into the kitchen and make her morning cup of tea. When Anurag surfaced, we made him clean half the living room with Dettol. Thirteen of us went for breakfast that morning and a large part of the time was spent mocking him for pissing on the chair. 'Anurag is our number one friend.' 'After his MBA he will join a company and they will make him the chairman.' They weren't the best jokes, but he was gracious enough to take them in his stride.

Pranks were a regular feature of our existence at the time. A friend of Sid's, a quiet fellow, Nitin, didn't want to celebrate his birthday. So a common friend hired a stripper. She came to the common friend's house and we made her wear a police woman's uniform. Ten minutes later, at about 7 p.m., she rang Nitin's doorbell. Over the intercom, she told him that she was a police officer. He let her in. When she got to the third floor where his flat was, she told him that his visa had expired and he was under arrest. She went into the house and handcuffed him. We stood outside the door and listened. After handcuffing Nitin, she removed his shirt. Then his trousers. Mortal fear turned to realisation and he shouted, 'Whatever they are paying you, I'll pay you double'. At this point, Nitin's flatmate let us all into the flat. I swear, had my friends ever played such a prank on me, I would have killed them. Imagine twenty people, boys and girls, in your living room, while you're on all fours, handcuffed, in only your underwear, with a stripper sitting on your back. She then proceeded to strip in front of him with this little audience watching. At one point, when she was topless and had dropped her pants, it was eerily silent. The silence clearly unnerved her a little so she said, 'Somebody say something'. Sid promptly responded, 'Nice underwear!'

One of the friends who was at this birthday 'surprise' was Rajiv Mehra. The poor guy had failed his UK driving test twice and was desperate to pass. He had spent a lot of money on lessons but just couldn't crack the practical test. I took only one lesson to understand what they tested you on and passed at first shot. He asked me how I had done it. I told him that I did it the Indian way. I registered for the test at the Shepard's Bush centre. While walking to the car with the examiner, I casually mentioned that in India we don't have to give a test and that £30 for the examiner normally does the trick. I then asked him whether that happened here in the UK too. He said £40 should do it. So I gave him £40, we went to McDonald's and I bought him a burger. He marked my sheet with mostly everything correct and a couple of minor mistakes so it would look genuine. And I passed my test.

Rajiv heard this story and immediately registered for his next driving test at the Shepard's Bush centre. He went there on a Saturday morning and tried to bribe the examiner. He was failed before he could get to the car and kicked out of the centre. The poor guy left feeling that his bribing skills were worse than his driving skills. I still haven't told him the truth. And yes, I'll take a one-way ticket to hell. First class, if you please.

On the subject of hell, this being a tough time in the job market, Shahin had lost his job and was home most of the time. I wasn't being placed on any projects, so most of the time I was 'working from home' as well. Working from home normally involved Shahin and me sitting in our pyjamas and watching Ally McBeal every afternoon. Sid, from upstairs, had also given up his job. One day, Sid and I had a long conversation about what his fake job description should be. If he was trying to flirt with girls, he would need to tell them he did something cool that would make them interested in him. We went through many options and weighed the pros and cons. Some options were automatically eliminated, e.g., he couldn't be a jockey because he wasn't light enough. Eventually we settled on 'author'. He had grown a beard and had the literary chops to pull it off.

That evening, Sid and I were drinking pints of Erdinger at a bar called Steam, next to Paddington station. Sid ended up in conversation with an attractive young Spanish girl. He was doing reasonably well, attempting to impress her with his rudimentary Spanish. Shahin, who was not privy to our earlier conversation, joined us. Exactly one minute later, Isabella asked Sid, 'So what do you do?' Sid replied very earnestly, 'I'm an author.' Shahin burst out laughing. And when I say burst, I mean the kind of burst when you've just taken a sip of beer and you laugh so hard the beer comes out of your mouth and nose at the same time. Needless to say, Isabella realised Sid was bullshitting and soon disappeared. Sid insisted that what Shahin did qualified as a 'buddy fuck' and demanded that he apologise. Shahin claimed in his defence that he wasn't aware of the back story, so there was no reason why he should. I did feel bad for Sid, but I know for sure 'the author' lived to write another chapter.

Kabir's job was not very stable either, at the time. One day he was working on his CV and asked me to help him with it. Now, like most men with an eleven-inch penis, I'm not very good at the art of embellishment, but I offered to help anyway. Kabir's father used to own a company in Calcutta that manufactured and delivered ice to people's houses. Occasionally, when the boy who delivered the ice on his cycle rickshaw came late, Kabir would shout at him. That 'responsibility' neatly translated into 'Director Human Resources and Logistics for the Magic Ice Company'. I was also quite impressed to read on his CV that he had represented India in swimming at the Asian Games in 1996.

A drunken reunion in Dubai, where
Shahin and Kabir now live

But I asked him to remove it. When asked why, I told him that one important characteristic of a lie that you want to pull off is that it needs to be believable. There were no Asian Games in 1996!

Those years at The 171 were some of the most wonderful years of my life. They were incredibly challenging too. Shahin was unemployed for a long time and paying rent became difficult for him. I insisted that he did not need to move out and we'd find an additional person to pick up part of the tab. For all practical purposes, although I was getting paid by my company, I was largely unemployed too. I joked about having the best job in the world because I was getting paid to do nothing, but in my heart I didn't find it funny. I was an ambitious young man who coveted success. However, I wasn't learning anything new or progressing professionally and this was making me increasingly disillusioned with the corporate world and my place in it. The lack of productive work and any form of achievement or recognition was once again eroding my confidence and self-worth. As Al Pacino said in *Scent of a Woman*, 'There was a time I could see. And I have seen. Boys like these, younger than these, their arms torn out, their legs ripped off. But there is nothin' like the sight...of an amputated spirit. There is no prosthetic for that. You think you're merely sendin' this splendid foot soldier...back home to Oregon with his tail between his legs, but I say you are...executin' his soul!'

Bit by bit, my job was hacking away at my very soul. The spirit and the dreams of the twenty-three-year-old boy who walked into the offices of IBM UK Ltd on the morning of 6 December 2000 with a crisply ironed shirt and shoes shining so bright you could see your face in them, were dying. Yet, in this time of soul-destroying helplessness, within the four walls of a three-bedroom flat in London, three friends propped each other up and filled the holes that had been burned in their souls. Sometimes with Sangria, but mostly with friendship.

rebirth

By the end of 2003, I was brain fried at IBM. I was a non-tech guy working in what was essentially an IT company. It was not my scene. Like a WWE wrestler at a synchronised swimming event, I was a fish out of water. However hard I tried, I just couldn't get my head around the technical stuff.

The grapevine had it that due to tough market conditions, sabbaticals were being offered at the company. You could take up to a year off and have your job waiting for you when you came back. And if you met certain criteria or had a strong case for a sabbatical, the company might even give you a small percentage of your salary while you were away. I went to my boss and told him I was interested in taking a sabbatical. He refused point blank. He said we were a small team with limited resources and I was required to stay. Since my work included conducting recruitment interviews for IBM, I had friends in Human Resources. I contacted an HR partner and got the precise list of criteria that IBM was looking for when granting sabbaticals. I went to my boss, shared the list with him, sold him on the idea, and we both took a sabbatical! What's more, given that my business case for a sabbatical was mysteriously aligned to IBM's criteria for approving one, I made the top bracket and was granted one year off on thirty-five per cent pay!

I started my sabbatical in early 2004. In February, I went backpacking with Sid in the beautiful state of Kerala. We did Kochi, Munnar, Thekkady (Periyar), Kumarakom, Allepey and finally Varkala. We didn't have a fixed plan and were just flying by the seat of our pants. When we reached Kumarakom, we confidently walked into the lobby of the Taj Hotel and asked them how much it cost for a room. The lady said nine thousand rupees. We explained that we didn't want to buy the room, just rent it for one night. After being escorted out by security, we found a shack where we got dinner, a bed to sleep, and breakfast by the lake for the grand sum of six hundred rupees. The

Sid and I in Varkala. February 2004

place also had wonderful hammocks and mosquitoes so big you'd need anti-aircraft guns to shoot them down. On that trip, we enjoyed the tea gardens of Munnar, the oily ayurvedic massages at Thekkady and the boat safari at the Periyar Wildlife Sanctuary. Our favourite place, however, was Varkala. A six-hundred-metre stretch of pristine beach, a cliff next to it with fifty restaurants and bars above, and cheap places to stay just behind them. From our bedroom window we could see the sea. The local fishermen willingly took us out on their boats in the morning so we could spot dolphins.

In April 2004, I went on a trek to Everest base camp. A few days into the trek, my cousin Dhruv, who was on the trek with me, got a very bad case of altitude sickness. He needed to be escorted back. Since my body hadn't acclimatised very well either, I offered to go down with him. Our last camp was the monastery town of Tengboche. Dhruv was put on a mule and I walked alongside, down to Namche Bazaar. At Namche, Dhruv was injected with fluids and then we took a helicopter down to Kathmandu. As soon as we reached Kathmandu, Dhruv felt perfectly fine. However, we were now presented with a unique dilemma. The Everest base camp trek was a high-altitude trek and as far as the world was concerned, we would not be contactable for the next six days. What, oh what, could we do with this opportunity, a six-day 'hall pass' if you will?

I tried my best to convince Dhruv that a trip to Thailand was a fantastic idea. He was one hundred per cent sure his wife would murder him if she ever got wind of it. So we settled instead for a four-days-and-three-nights 'casino package' at a fancy hotel in Kathmandu. We checked into our luxurious hotel, thrilled to not be sleeping in tents. I lay on the bed and turned on the TV and Dhruv went to the loo. One minute later, the phone rang. I answered. It was Dhruv's wife. I pretended I could not hear and hung up. Then I ran to knock on the bathroom door and inform Dhruv. 'WHAT!' he shrieked. I'm quite sure if he was sitting on the pot, he must have stood up. 'I'm dead,' he said, 'I'm dead.' It turned out a nephew of Dhruv's wife was to have come on the trek with us. He couldn't make it because he was unwell just before. To make up for it, his parents thought they'd bring him to Kathmandu for a few days. So they called up our trekking agency to enquire about nice places to stay. The agency informed them that two trekkers were sick and had to be evacuated. Our secret was out.

The challenge Dhruv faced was how to stay on in Nepal and make the most of our famed 'casino package'. If he said that he was unwell, his wife would show up in Kathmandu the next day. If he said he was well, she would want him to return to Delhi immediately. Therefore, it was decided that I was unwell and not okay to fly, so he had to stay one more day to look after me. Had he said two or three days, she would have come. So, one day at a time, we bought time for us to spend the 11,000 chips we were given to use on the poker tables. I have since been given official black sheep status and Dhruv is no longer permitted to travel anywhere that he cannot be reached on a mobile phone. Incidentally, after this episode, we learnt of a medicine called Diamox that helps control altitude sickness. It allowed me in later years to trek up to Annapurna base camp and climb Mount Kilimanjaro.

Rebirth

In August that year, I went to the Edinburgh Fringe Festival where I was blown away watching stand-up comedy. I mean, here was a guy on stage, with a drink in one hand and a microphone in the other, just having fun. And that was his job! I told myself I had to had to do this. In fact, sometimes I joke that I got 'burnt' into comedy because I saw Jason Byrne, Brendon Burns and Ed Byrne, one after the other, and watching them inspired me to go forth and give it a go. I'm pleased to say that since then I've shared both drinks and stages with all three of these comedy giants.

When I started doing stand-up comedy, I was actually debating between doing a bartending course and getting into stand-up comedy. I thought both those professions were really cool but the bartending course that I looked up only taught one how to mix the drinks. They didn't teach how to juggle the glasses. I thought to myself, if I can't juggle the glasses, I'm never going to get laid. That's why I got into stand-up comedy. And that was fifteen years ago. In the last fifteen years I can't tell you how many times...how many times I wish I had taken that bartending course.

In September that same year, I enrolled myself in a comedy course in London. Most of my classmates were young white men who were not so subtle when mocking me and hinting that they thought I wasn't funny and didn't have any future in comedy. As fate would have it, none of those young men are in the comedy business today.

This is also when I took on the name 'Papa CJ'. I'd been called 'CJ' since I was sixteen. I couldn't use my legal name—try getting a white man to introduce a performer with an Indian name on stage! He might as well just call you

With Brendon Burns in Amsterdam. He said 'you know how good a comedian is when you have to follow him'. I learnt that when I followed Brendon at a late night gig in Edinburgh.

Dara Herlihy

With Ed Byrne, backstage at The Comedy Store. I have on occasion been called an Indian Ed Byrne. Clearly they were referring to the similarity in our looks and not our talent. I can only hope to be as good as he is one day.

With Jason Byrne when he toured India. There are few comedians on the planet who are as good at improvisation and crowd work as Jason. At a gig we once did together, I saw him do twenty minutes about the curtains in the room!

John. I've had people even screw up Papa CJ and introduce me as CJ Papa. At the time I took on the name Papa CJ, I hadn't put much thought into it. I know why it works in hindsight—it's catchy, easy to remember, works as a brand, and if anyone ever tries to come find 'Papa CJ' to stab him, he can only find someone by that name at a comedy club where there is security. More about that later.

At the time, since I was the only Indian comedian in all of the United Kingdom, I was doing a lot of material that aimed to project India in a positive light. So maybe subconsciously I thought to myself, *Angrezon ko lagna chahiye ki unka bhi koi baap hai* (the English should feel that somebody is their daddy too)! A postcolonial revolt.

Now, whenever I travel for shows, the first question I get asked at interviews is, 'What is your real name?' I don't like answering the question. I think people are desperately curious to know so they can mentally slot you into a box by identifying you as belonging to a certain community or background. So every time I am asked, I try and make up the biggest bullshit story I can to see if they will print it. One story I gave out was that when I was a teenager I saw a brutal mafia murder and since then, I have been under a witness protection programme run by the International Court of Justice. My own favourite answer, though, is this: 'I was born in Vatican City where it is customary to name a child after his or her physical characteristics. "Papa" is the literal translation of the Latin word "massivus" and "CJ" is the literal translation of the Latin word "genitalius".' This was actually printed in a newspaper.

Another interview I had fun with was in Chandigarh. I was doing a show there in 2009 as part of a national tour.

As I drove down from the mountains, a young journalist kept calling me for an interview. I told her I'd call her back as soon as I reached the city. When I did, she opened with, 'My editor has asked me to interview you but I don't know what you do.' 'I'm a professional pole dancer,' I replied. I gave her a twenty-minute interview on pole dancing. She called back with clarifying questions. The following day, three newspapers in Chandigarh wrote about how I would be performing stand-up comedy at the Chandigarh Golf Club. The front page of the *Tribune* however, had an article titled 'Poles Apart'.

...Poles apart
Papa CJ has no qualms about pole dancing

For the Indian audinece, Malaika Arora Khan gyrationg around the pole in Kaante made for an uneasy watch. Recently, the three hunks of Bollywood - Akshay Kumar, Fardeen Khan and Ritesh Deshmukh dancing sensuality around a vertical pole in Heyy Baby , made women gawk and blush in hushed admiration. Men pole dancing! Never heard of it. But, we would certainly want to know about someone who boasts of this gyrating proficiency. Meet Papa CJ, pole dancer and stand up comedian from Kolkata now settled in London, in the city to perform at Golf Club. Perform, we bet you would end up scandalising people. "I don't know," he says. "I don't have inhibitions. Let's see," he adds.

Pole dancing, why would someone want to zero in on this whacky, awkward professions? "I was doing a corporate job, and I happened to see men pole dancers at a night club in London. I thought it was a wow profession, and I moved over to it. Now, this is what I do full time, " he says with ease as opposed to an uncomfortable expression on our face. Reactions from the family, the first thing that comes to our mind. Offers Papa CJ, "They were shocked. However, now they have accepted it and they support me too." We still can't separate pole dancing from the smoky, naughty environment of the night clubs. "When I performed in Delhi, people were uncomfortable, in Kolkata they were scandalised, while I got a great response in Pune," he adds. More on the moves and how he does it? "First, I begin with chatting up the audiences. Later on, when I see they are comfortable, I start with pole dancing, where I invite women to take off the two layers of my clothes." And how does he deal with those uncomfortable, shocked looks? "The trick is to switch off the lights," says CJ. "Two drinks down, and lights off, uneasiness vanishes in the air."

It's not my fault if people don't do their research!

Back to the name thing, though. My real name is Chirag Jain. Don't worry, I can understand the disappointment. Papa CJ can lead an army into battle. Chirag Jain can feed them food when they come back. That, too, vegetarian food with no onions. Papa CJ can take three women to a hotel and have a foursome and leave. Chirag Jain probably owns the hotel and can give them a forty per cent discount. The women love Papa CJ. The women also love Chirag Jain... but not like that. 'But not like that' = no sex for you, EVER.

Towards the end of October 2004, I was on stage for the first time. The first gig I was officially booked to do was on a boat on the river Thames, called the Wibbley Wobbley Boat. The Wibbley Wobbley was known to be a tough gig, but I got a decent number of laughs and escaped fairly unscathed. My set was preceded by Malcolm Hardee's traditional introduction, 'This next guy's probably going to be shit. Please welcome, Papa CJ'. This was the same infamous Malcolm Hardee who was known to have urinated on the head of an audience member who fell asleep in the first row at a gig. His risqué pranks were legendary and he was famous for having stolen Freddie Mercury's £4000 fortieth birthday cake. His advice to comics who were concerned that a joke might be offensive to an audience was: 'If you think it's funny, then fuck 'em'.

The only comedian on the circuit who compared in notoriety to Malcolm was circuit legend Ian Cognito. 'Cogs', as he was called, was as dangerous on stage as he was kind and docile off it. He was known as Britain's 'most banned' comic and one of the most famous parts of his act involved bringing a hammer on stage, banging a nail into a wall and hanging a hat off it, followed by the lines, 'This lets you know two things about me…firstly, I really don't give a shit. Secondly, I've got a hammer.' I gigged with him on my third ever gig, at the Cheeky Monkey in Birmingham, and felt like I had been hit by a hurricane.

The way progression worked on the UK comedy circuit was that as an open micer (new comedian), you started with a five-minute set. Then you moved to seven, ten, occasionally fifteen, and then twenty. In most cases, it was a jump straight from ten to twenty. I say jump, but if you're a new comedian, you will know that it is not a jump but a colossal leap. You could spend months creating a ten-minute set that works, impress a booker and have them invite you to do a paid twenty at their club…when you have no more than eleven or twelve minutes of material that you know works! It's a conundrum many a comedian has faced and will continue to face. Do you tell them that you're not ready and risk not being called back for years? Or do you accept and try and come up with twenty by the time you hit their club—once again taking the risk that you might die and never be called back again?

In my early days in comedy, I was probably one of the hardest working comedians in the UK, along with Patrick Monahan. I gigged every day. Not almost every day, EVERY day. In April 2005, I did thirty-five gigs and that's because I cancelled a few. On a three-day trip to Manchester, I did six gigs. I remember that after one of these, the comedian who was driving me back to London was so stressed on account of his performance that he did a line of cocaine off the hood of his car before starting the drive down. Yes, in those days there was a risk of dying off stage as well! (For the civilians, when nobody is laughing at your jokes, it's called bombing or dying on stage. On the other hand, when you're doing really well, it's often called killing or destroying. On principle we try and keep very peaceful terminology in our industry.)

You might think that six gigs in three days is not much to talk about, but when you're a new act on a circuit with 500 open micers vying for the same five-minute spot at a comedy club, I promise you it requires a serious amount of hustling to get those many dates in the diary. When I say 'hustle' I mean a little bit of talent (or maybe just a little more than a little) and a large amount of grovelling. I did 250 gigs in my first ten months. 700 in my first three years. That's a lot of grovelling.

As an open micer on the London circuit, there were two ways to get gigs. You could open the *Time Out* magazine and see which clubs were offering open spots. Notice I said 'open' the magazine and not buy it. I'd always just open the magazine at a newsagent's shop, write down the info I needed, and put the magazine back on the shelf. Or you could talk to other open micers and find out where the gigs were and how one could get a spot.

There were out-of-town gigs and London gigs. The out-of-town ones were normally nicer because you'd be the middle spot, doing up to ten minutes, to a reasonably large crowd (anywhere up to 400 people). However, you'd often have to spend over ten hours on the road to do that ten-minute spot. I remember driving all the way to Durham once, a six- or seven-hour journey one way, to do a university gig. The comedian travelling with me was deaf, so you can imagine how much conversation we had to keep ourselves entertained. We reached there to find that the students had exams and only three kids had showed up for the gig. We had been on the road for seven hours to get there, so you bet your ass we performed!

The London gigs, on the other hand, were a different breed. You had no idea of the quality of the gig or the size of the audience. More often than not, open mic nights had more comedians than audience members. There were some rooms that were always nice. Like Downstairs at The King's Head at Crouch End. A lovely gig in a room with low ceilings and a light that shone right above your head. At almost every gig I've done there, whether or not anyone has come and spoken to me about what they thought of the quality of my performance, one or more women have come up and asked me which shampoo I use. My hair isn't that nice, it was the lights, but thanks for the compliment anyway, dear objectifiers!

A lot of the London gigs were around Soho, which had at least twelve venues within a two-kilometre radius. One of these was Big Night Out, which had two gigs in a pub on Oxendon Street. One in the basement and one on the first floor. I was once booked to do both gigs there on the same night. And I learnt a valuable lesson. I first played the basement, which I absolutely destroyed. It didn't strike me at the time that, as a performer, you build momentum over the course of a gig. At the start, if you're an unknown, you need to win over the crowd. Once you do, they grant you the right to be a cocky little shit by the end. Not realising this, I walked off after destroying the basement to do the middle spot on the first floor. The adrenaline was pumping and I started my set to the new audience as a cocky little shit—without first proving that I was funny. They, of course, were having none of it, and I died on my arse.

As a new comic on the London circuit, there were three people you wanted to impress. First and foremost, Don Ward. Owner of The Comedy Store, the most prestigious comedy club in the UK and the hardest to get into. Getting a weekend at the Store announced your arrival as comedy royalty. I practically lived at the Store in my early days of comedy, watching as many acts as I possibly could. I still believe it's one of the best comedy clubs in the world. And

Dara Herlihy

the staff there were wonderful—from Alex Rochford and Simon in the sound box to Kim and everyone else who worked at the bar, and big Mark and Julian, the bouncers who worked the door.

The first time I went to The Comedy Store was on Monday, 25 October 2004. My friend Pete was performing at The King Gong show and a few of us went to support him. The King Gong is a show hosted by a professional comedian, where about twenty-five new comedians take the stage and their aim is to TRY and last five minutes. The audience is told that if they like the comedian, they should clap and cheer, and if they don't, they are welcome to heckle and boo. Three people in the audience are randomly given red cards and appointed judges. If they don't like a comedian or feel the crowd doesn't, they raise the red card and the comedian gets 'gonged' off.

The host riles the crowd into a frenzy before the show begins. It's brutal. On average, a comedian lasts ninety seconds. I've never seen more than five comedians get through five minutes. It's normally two or three. At the end, from among the comedians who made it through five minutes, the audience cheers for the one they liked the most, and that comedian is pronounced King of the Gong.

The real prize, however, other than every open micer on the circuit finding out who won, is that you get noticed by Don Ward, and if he thinks your material is half decent, you get invited to do a five-minute open spot on a Thursday night on the early show. That honour doesn't let you sleep all night because you want to call their office first thing in the morning and book a spot. Of course, when you call Charlotte or Simon or Alex, you realise that the next available five-minute spot on a Thursday is eight months away!

What I didn't know when we went to see Pete was that in the middle of the King Gong show, the MC asks the audience if any of them would like to give it a go. This happened during the first half of the show. And I thought, what the hell, I'm going to give it a shot. I had been writing some jokes in preparation for my first official open spot, and I thought there really could be no downside. I knocked back two Jack Daniels and volunteered to get on stage in the second half. I don't remember how the time flew when I took the stage but I remember hearing the 'Hallelujah' soundtrack when I finished five minutes on stage...and if that wasn't surprise enough, at the end of the night, I won! I have done the King Gong twelve times since and hold a record for never being gonged off. I also won the show ten times, including once at The Comedy Store in Manchester.

The second person one wanted to impress on the circuit was Geoff Whiting. He ran a comedy empire by the name of Mirth Control Comedy. I say 'empire' because at one point he was booking 111 rooms all over the country. One hundred and eleven! If he saw you and liked you, theoretically he could put you on stage every night of the week. Geoff himself MC-ed quite a few gigs, so ideally you wanted to be on one of those, so he could see you live.

Geoff saw me for the first time at my third ever gig. It was at London Metropolitan University on Holloway Road. He was hosting the show and luckily for me, I did well. Over the next three years, I did maybe 300 gigs for Mirth

Control. The first money I got paid was at one of their gigs. I wasn't supposed to be paid. It was my ninth ever gig in a pub in a hole-in-the-wall village about three hours' drive from London. The pub owner liked my set and gave me a £10 tip! After a while, when I started doing well at most of the gigs, I demanded that I get paid and not perform for free each time. Eventually I did start getting paid and while the money was never great (I'm talking £40 to £75), I got something more valuable from the Mirth Control gigs. In the three years that I performed in the UK, I must have spent over 2000 hours in cars with over 500 comedians who had been doing comedy for fifteen or twenty years. I saw how they prepared, I saw how they worked a room, I heard them analyse their performances afterwards and I begged them to see my set and give me feedback. That was Comedy University right there.

The one thing with Geoff's gigs was that you never knew what it would be like until you got there. He always sold it to you as a 'lovely room', but that wasn't always the case. I remember showing up at a gig in Birgmingham where it turned out the show was in an Asian wedding hall, with a stage that had two velvet chairs. The closest of the ten round tables was fifty feet away and the microphone was faulty. I ended up walking up to the first table, ripping off the tablecloth, standing on the table and belting out my set from there without a microphone.

Another gig I showed up at was in Leicester. Leicester, if you don't know, is two hours' drive from London and has a large brown and black population. I got to the venue and found that it was adjacent to a mosque. Ramzan had just finished, people had said their prayers, eaten their food and come for a stand-up comedy show. I asked the organiser if there were any suggested restrictions on language or content because I wanted to make sure that I was respectful of the surroundings and the occasion. He said, 'No no, I have seen what you do, they know what they are coming for, you go for it.'

So I went for it. I was closing my show with some material about eating pussy. Adjacent to a mosque. And at the back of the room I could see a guy indicating 'cut, cut' with a hand gesture across his throat. I thought to myself, you're not the director, so I carried on and finished my set. Ninety-nine per cent of the audience loved it but one per cent of the Asian elders got upset.

After the show, when I went to the bathroom, three guys showed up with knives (I am talking nine-inch-blade knives) and offered to stab me. I mean, it wasn't exactly an offer. They weren't posh English people saying, 'If you don't mind, could I possibly stab you?' It was a lot more aggressive than that. I told them I had specifically taken permission from the organiser for the content and that they should go and speak to him. If he disagreed, they were welcome to come back and do whatever they liked to me. Luckily for me, all three guys went to speak to the organiser. I quickly ran out, got into my car, and drove speedily back to London.

The following week, on a Friday afternoon, I got a call from the Leicestershire police.

Hello. Is that Papa CJ?

Yes.

This is PC Ranveer calling from Leicestershire police.

Yes, officer.

Did you do a gig adjacent to a mosque in Leicester last week?

Yes, officer, I did.

At this point I am shitting myself because I have no clue what he is going to charge me with. In the UK they have laws around inciting racial hatred, etc.

Did you close your set with material on cunnilingus?

Errr…yes, officer, I did.

All right. Three hundred black and Asian officers are having their Christmas party tonight. We would really like you to come and perform.

That was the Leicestershire police. I remember another incident in London. We had finished a late show in Soho. Five comedians got into a car afterwards, at around 3 a.m. Now, I do not endorse drinking and driving, but this is what happened. The driver mistakenly drove the wrong way into a one-way lane, the cops started trailing us, and pulled us over. When they checked the driver, he was over the permissible alcohol limit. The law in the UK says you need to be tested at the car and then at the police station as well. And if you're above the limit, it's a pretty serious offence.

The car was parked on the side of the road and the driver was shoved into the cop van. As moral support, we offered to go along. On the way to the police station, we started chatting with the police. They were clearly looking for illegal mini-cab drivers. We told them we were comedians and that we had just finished a show. We were trying to encourage the audience to have a few drinks, so we had to show them that we were having a few ourselves. The cops in our van were from Scotland, so we spoke to them about the Edinburgh Festival. To cut a long story short, we ended up performing for the police, in the police station, from 4 a.m. to 6 a.m. Meanwhile, they got the driver something to eat, gave him water to drink, let him go to the bathroom and breath-tested him again at 6.30 a.m. By that time, he was below the limit. 'Sorry to trouble you sir, the first machine must have been faulty. You are free to go!' Now that, my friends, is 'epic'!

The third lot you wanted to impress were the folk who ran a chain of clubs called Jongleurs. They ran clubs across the country and you got paid upwards of £150 per show for a twenty-minute set. If they booked you for a weekend, you had hit the jackpot. It meant a gig on Thursday, one on Friday, one on Saturday, and one on Sunday. Some clubs had two gigs on Saturdays and, if I remember correctly, Leeds may even have had two gigs on a Friday. In comedy terms, that was a LOT of money. And they gave you a hotel room for the weekend. Far from a glamorous hotel, but a hotel nonetheless. If you got in with Jongleurs, you could make a living doing stand-up. I use the word 'living' very loosely, but it was good money. Where's the catch, you ask. Well, here it is. What Jongleurs wanted more than anything was an act that was reliable, i.e., would consistently deliver a solid performance. However, Jongleurs gigs were not easy to play. Some of the rooms were lovely, but some were not. The format on most nights was this: MC at the top, act one, MC for five minutes, act two, interval. Then the MC again, open spot or middle act, MC for five minutes, and then the headliner. Then—and this is why it was a tough gig—they'd take away all the chairs and it would become a DJ and disco night. So, very often, you'd get people who hadn't come for comedy. They'd come to get shitfaced with alcohol and dance and try and get laid afterwards. You'd get a bunch of hen and stag nights, with folks not interested in listening to the comedy at all. And even if they were, to start with, they would get so drunk that they had the attention span of amoeba. And these were rooms where you had hecklers—both coherent and incoherent. What this meant was that as a comedian, you had to be able to do two things. You had to be able to deliver a punchline every twenty seconds to hold their attention. And you had to learn how to deal with hecklers and command the attention of a rough room. It was like taming a wild tiger.

I remember a particularly rough night in Cardiff when the air-conditioning wasn't working, they had two stag nights in, four hen nights, one work outing of forty-five female prison wardens, and the world cup football playing on the television at the back of the room! It was a gig from hell. I struggled doing my spot. In the break, the bouncers kicked out the prison wardens for being too disruptive. The brilliant Jeff Innocent, who was headlining, stopped fifteen minutes into his set, put the microphone back in the stand and said, 'You guys aren't worth it' and walked off stage.

I did my first five-minute open spot for Jongleurs Camden in London in June 2005. I had won the Gong show a few times in London by then, I sent them a video, and they called me to do a spot. There were two people who handled booking for Jongleurs, Rosie and Donna. As luck would have it, Donna was in the room that night and saw me perform. Having done the Gong so many times, I was able to not only handle the boisterous crowd but also deliver a solid set. The next thing I knew, they asked me to do a paid fifteen. Holy hell! I told Donna I didn't have a fifteen that I was confident I could deliver to a Jongleurs crowd, and so, the next time, they gave me a paid ten. Nine months into comedy, a chain that could take years to break into had started giving me paid work! I'm incredibly grateful for these gigs I got—even the shitty ones. They gave me money when there was none around, a thick skin when they kicked my arse, and a lot of learning—not only by watching other comedians work those rooms but also by learning how to work them myself. I went on to play almost every single one of their clubs across the country and between Jongleurs and Mirth Control, I've performed at more than sixty towns and cities across the UK. I love flying into London and seeing the map that is telecast on the little TV screen on the plane. I get a kick from seeing that I have performed in every single city that is shown on that map.

From the little I understand of what is happening on the UK circuit right now, I believe that TV comedy and the likes of Netflix have caused the live circuit to implode somewhat. People are either not stepping out for live stand-up or, if they do, they want to see the guys they've seen on TV. This is making it hard for new comics trying to go up the ranks to get live work. Fortunately for them, they have the internet—a democracy where anyone with talent can get noticed immediately. Sadly, the internet doesn't put you through the kind of hard yards that stage time does. A five-minute clip that gets five million online views might enable you to sell out a 500-seater theatre, but it won't teach you how to hold an audience's attention for an hour once they are in the room. I feel incredibly fortunate to have been on the circuit at a time when it was possible as a new act to gig every single day of the year.

As you might expect, getting on the radar of the influencers and bookers of comedy was very difficult for a new act. One way to do it was to enter new act competitions and make it to later rounds where the who's who of comedy would be invited as judges, including club owners, agents, TV personalities and maybe some media. I entered a bunch of competitions. I made it to the finals of the Laughing Horse competition, the semi-finals of So You Think You're Funny where I died a terrible death in Edinburgh, the Newbury Comedy Competition which I won and got a £500 cheque for, the BBC new act competition where I struggled while performing on a boat called Tattershall Castle on the River Thames, and the Hackney Empire New Act Competition in which I was placed third.

The Hackney Empire competition is held in a venue of the same name, a beautiful 1275-capacity space with a rich legacy. The likes of Charlie Chaplin have performed there. It's in what a London property agent would call a 'vibrant' neighbourhood, which is their way of saying you could get stabbed on the street. One of the upsides of being placed in the top three at their new act competition was that they would produce a show and take you to Edinburgh. Henning Vehn, Lee Nelson and I were offered a triple header show at a room in the Gilded Balloon at the Edinburgh Fringe in August 2005. We said yes.

I could write another book on what a young comic learns when he or she goes to the Edinburgh Fringe Festival as a performer. It is both an exciting and a terrifying place to be. Exciting for all the things you see and learn, and the people you meet. And terrifying for how difficult it is, and realising how little you know and how insignificant you are. The Fringe has over 3000 shows per day, around 700 of which are comedy, and you are competing against all of them for an audience. You've spent money on accommodation, the venue, posters, flyers, ticketing, entry into the Fringe brochure, PR…a lot of money is on the line and there is a near impossible chance of recovering it. Rumour has it that the average Fringe audience size is in single digits. So you're out on the street for hours on end, distributing flyers for your show to people who do not want another flyer thrown in their face, hoping they will show up. You want the media to attend your show, yet you're terrified of getting a bad review that will make your sales worse than they already are. Most of your fellow comedians are highly strung because they are stressed, losing money, consuming unhealthy food and vast quantities of alcohol and sometimes performing four-five short spots on mixed bill shows to promote their solo shows. Shows start at 9 a.m. and go on till 3 a.m., so, depending on the time slots you get, it can be an exhausting day.

All the above said, the Fringe is a magical place to be. You can see performers from all parts of the world in a range of art forms. The best in the world and the guys just starting out. There are expensive tickets, reasonably priced tickets and free shows. The Royal Mile in Edinburgh has street performers, magicians, jugglers and all sorts of other acts showcasing their stuff. As a registered performer, you get access to the performers' bars which stay open till 5 a.m. and get to hang out with colleagues you have worked with through the year, as well as hobnob with industry people and comedy royalty. You get to see the very best in your field and how they ply their craft. If you can wangle it, you get to perform on multiple mixed bill shows to large audiences. You learn to tailor your material to cater to people from different countries and leave the festival a better comedian. Tired, but better.

My favourites of all the Fringe shows have always been the late night ones. There is a show called Spank which starts at midnight and goes on till 4 a.m. The first ninety minutes are comedy, with a break in the middle, and then the room becomes a night club. It has low ceilings, black walls, a small stage, and can fit in about 200 people stuffed together. The hosts get on stage and tell the audience that there are three rules of Spank. The first rule is that whenever

anyone on stage says the word 'spank', the audience needs to shout, 'You love it'. It's a late gig, so this helps get the energy going. The second rule is that everyone has to drink alcohol. And the third rule is, when the comedy ends and the music starts, everyone has to 'make out' with someone. Those are the rules! Which is why they say, 'What happens at the festival stays at the festival'. Except, of course, sexually transmitted diseases!

When the second half of the comedy begins, if you are in the audience and have a show that you'd like to promote, you're allowed to come on stage and tell the audience about it. Spank is a popular gig, so it's a good way to get word-of-mouth going. And there are always several other performers in the audience. So you can get on stage and promote your show, but the rule is, you have to be naked. Completely naked. It's called 'the naked promo'. They put on music, you dance, take your clothes off, and that gives you one minute on the microphone to promote your show. Then they take your flyer and stick it on the wall and the show carries on. You can imagine how I feel when I'm performing in India and someone asks me whether comedy shows here are censored as compared to those abroad!

Another legendary late night show at the Fringe is Late 'n' Live. The very mention of Late 'n' Live is enough to send a chill down the spine of a comedian, no matter how experienced or reputed. This legendary bear pit of a gig, kicking off at 1 a.m., has welcomed many established comics onto its stage. It is the best late night hang out where anything can happen...and probably will. Celebrity guests and local and international comedy favourites get up every night to tackle the rowdy crowd and MANY fail.

At my first festival as a performer, in August 2005, I was told never to try doing Late 'n' Live as it was really difficult and could only damage one's reputation. But, of course, nothing excites me more than a challenge! Nine months after my first gig, on the final weekend of the Fringe, my friend Stephen K. Amos, who was compering the gig, agreed to sneak me on after the first act, to do five minutes. For context, Stephen K. Amos is a lovely man and a hilarious comedian. A week before this gig, there was a fire alarm at the Gilded Balloon where he had a solo show. He dragged his 200-plus audience outside and while they were waiting, on Stephen's request, I entertained them in the open courtyard that is Bristo Square. Like a street performer with a circle around me, I belted out jokes at the top of my lungs.

Back to Late 'n' Live. The organiser found out about our little deal and after much negotiation we agreed on the following—I would get four minutes plus one minute for every round of applause I got. The gig started, it was a full house, the audience was rowdy and heaving, and the first act struggled. I was bumped down the order and the second act, a double act, also went on and struggled. The organiser apologised for not being able to put me on and said he needed to put the headliner on immediately, so maybe next year. The third act was on stage and not exactly storming the gig and the crowd hadn't got their money's worth. After much convincing by Amos, who kept telling Ged, the organiser, 'This guy has jokes', he agreed to let me on after the last act. Rob Deering, also a comedian, who would be playing in the band afterwards, agreed that if I struggled he would do a few jokes before kicking off the music.

Dara Herlihy

After the third act, Amos introduced me and got me on stage. A true rock and roll stage. I was immediately engulfed by bright lights and the excitement and fear that only a first-timer on a rowdy Late 'n' Live would understand. Established comedians tremble at this gig and here I was, nine months after my first gig, attempting to close the show on the final weekend! I threw out my first line, and got a round of applause. I'm in, I thought…and I have one extra minute! I ended up doing ten minutes that night and had a storming set. I couldn't sleep till 9 a.m. the following day. A definite peak in the fledgling career of young Papa CJ.

Note: I was officially booked to do Late 'n' Live a couple of years later. I followed Brendon Burns that night and I died on my arse!

Six months into my sabbatical, I applied for a raise, which to my surprise was sanctioned. When my one-year sabbatical was almost complete, I applied for a three-month extension, which was approved. I then applied for another three-month extension, which I was granted. Then I heard the company was giving people severance packages (a pot of money to leave the company), so I cancelled my last extension and went back to work on full pay. And then I applied for, and was granted, a severance package. I was told to work in a particular department for the duration of my six-week notice period. However, I managed to convince my new boss that anything I worked on would be left unfinished, so it was best I did no work at all. Oh, happy days!

A year into doing stand-up comedy full time, I was dead broke. So I applied for a job and got one working for a recruitment firm in Covent Garden. It was a wonderful place to work in. There were maybe fifteen of us and the average age was around twenty-five. I was asked to head the consulting desk. I worked with two wonderful people, Joanna and Graeme. We had a table tennis table in the office and I spent a decent amount of time in the TT room. I remember, while I was playing table tennis during a break, my boss came in and asked me why I wasn't working. I took him into the office, showed him that my billing numbers were the highest in the firm and told him to only disturb me when they came down. He was a good guy, though, and gave me the flexibility to pursue my comedy as long as my work didn't suffer. I would work in the day and perform at night, and if I had an out-of-town gig, I would come in late the following day. The truth is that I worked really hard. I hustled. This was before the word hustle became fashionable. You know how you can go to a restaurant and drop your business card in a bowl and maybe win a free meal? I used to go to restaurants, steal those cards when nobody was looking, cold call those people and place them in jobs. My hustle extended to my comedy life as well. If I was ever at an airport, I would go to the business centre, get on every single computer terminal, open the browser and change the home page to www.papacj.com.

One of my recruitment firm clients was a company called The Mind Gym. They were, and still are, in the business of executive coaching. Half the employees were psychologists who developed training courses and the other half were change consultants who sold these 'workouts' to clients. The coaches themselves were part of a freelance network. One day, I decided to leave my firm and qualify as a coach with them. The gig was a good one. I'd tell them my free dates and ask them to get me work. Or they'd send out a mail saying a session was available and we could apply to deliver it. It was a great way to support my comedy habit. It could be the additional source of income I needed to stay afloat. What's more, I really enjoyed the work. I was happy to do any workout, for any client, in any country, at any seniority level, on short notice. So I became one of their most prolific coaches. I ran over hundred sessions for The Mind Gym and my clients included Nike, Google and UBS in Europe, Accenture, E&Y and Deutsche Bank in America, Universal Music and BBC in the UK, and HSBC and Unilever in India. Once, after running a coaching session for Diesel, the marketing head told me I could go to their Regent Street store in London the next day and buy anything I wanted at an employee discount of forty-seven per cent. I went to the store very excited, only to discover that even with a forty-seven per cent discount, I couldn't afford anything they had!

Occasionally I did get the odd decently paying gig. In May 2007, I hosted the Citywealth Magic Circle awards at the London Zoo. Top European private bankers and their ultra high net worth clients were in attendance. The organisers were to arrange for me to be picked up, as a guest of honour. As it happens, the event was sponsored by Maybach. Now, for those of you who haven't heard of Maybach, let me fill you in. Maybach is a direct competitor of Rolls Royce, and the car that I got picked up in, the Maybach 62, had that same week been in the services of Dr Vijay Mallya and P. Diddy. Like a little child, I couldn't decide whether I'd rather lounge in the back like a king or go up in the front seat next to the drive and explore the controls of Starship Enterprise!

The irony was that Maybach was only sponsoring pickups. So while this struggling artist was picked up in a $400,000 piece of machinery, he had to sneak out later when no one was looking and catch the night bus home! Not that a London bus is a cheap piece of machinery. It's also bigger than the Maybach 62 and I don't know a single individual who owns one. I also took back leftover food from the event in a doggy bag. Yes, I know—classy!

Among other things, I once did a show in London for the Women's India Association of the UK. The negotiation was most interesting. After all the logical reasons for asking me to lower my fee had been exhausted, the lady at the other end of the phone said, 'But beta (son), I am like your mother'! It occurred to me that I wouldn't be surprised if this line of 'argument' had been used in other situations as well. Like buying a flat.

Madam, this property is for 500,000.

I'll give you 5000. (Yes, that really is how they negotiate).

I'm sorry madam, but that is what the fair market price is.

But beta, I am like your mother!

And it doesn't matter if they are buying or selling. You could go to a strip club and have this conversation:

Lady, how much for a lap dance?

One hundred pounds.

Can you not do it for fifty?

But beta…

Somehow, we found middle ground and I agreed to do the show in a fancy hotel in Knightsbridge in London. As part of the event, I was asked to host an auction as well. I always try and make these auctions a competitive affair by turning it into a battle of the sexes. One of the items that came up for bidding was a small 2x3 feet painting. The two competing parties in this bid ended up being a certain Mr Gupta and Mrs Usha Mittal, Laxmi Mittal's wife. She was seated at the first table with Lord Swraj Paul and Mrs Sarah Jane Brown, wife of the then British prime minister, Gordon Brown. (If, for some reason, you live under a rock and don't know who Laxmi Mittal is, he is the owner of Arcelor Steel and the richest Indian in the UK, with a net worth in excess of $10 billion. That is enough money to buy a semi-luxurious 1.5 bedroom apartment just off Marine Drive in South Mumbai.)

The opening bid of £1000 came from Mrs Mittal. The way I was running the auction, I would announce each bidder's name and bid and get the audience to give them a round of applause (you'd be surprised how much more people will spend when their egos are appropriately massaged). So after she said £1000, I said, 'What is your name, madam?' Instantly, I had 400 of the who's who of London staring at me thinking, 'You idiot! Surely you know who she is?'

Mrs Mittal responded, 'Usha.'

I asked in search of a surname, 'Usha what?'

She said, 'Just Usha.'

I announced, 'Ladies and gentlemen, we have a bid of £1000 by Mrs Usha Mittal, please give her a round of applause.'

As the audience applauded, I could sense her thinking, 'You bastard. You knew my name all this while!'

Mr Gupta then bid £1100. She bid £1500. He said £1600. She said £2000. He said £2100. I mocked him for playing blind while Mrs Mittal was playing chaals. Eventually Mrs Mittal won at £2500 and I asked the audience to give her a big round of applause. Now here's the fun part. While 400 people were applauding, Laxmi Mittal whispered to me from the side, 'Is delivery included?' I waited for the applause to die down and announced to the audience, 'Ladies and gentlemen, this is how you get to the top. Mr Laxmi Mittal wants to know whether delivery is included.' As the audience laughed and clapped, Laxmi Mittal picked up the napkin from his table and covered his face. However, due credit to him, he took the joke in his stride and we shook hands before he left. Of course, he's never invited me to perform for him, but that's probably because in addition to my performance fee, my clients also have to pay for my travel, boarding and lodging. #DeliveryNotIncluded.

By this time, I had got myself an agent in London. A wonderful young man by the name of Brett Vincent. He had worked with another agency before and was now setting up his own shop. Having seen my work at The Comedy Store, he decided to take a chance on me, as I did on him! In case you're wondering, no, we didn't sign a contract. It was a gentleman's handshake that has held firm till date.

Thanks to Brett, I got to do a bit of international work. He took me to Malta for a wonderful weekend of gigs. He also organised for me to do a bunch of gigs in the French Alps. Since my dad was visiting at the time, I took him along too. It was a pretty sweet deal. An all-expenses paid trip to live in a chalet and do twenty minutes a night in different ski resorts. We also got free ski lessons, although the girl who volunteered to teach us was perennially drunk, even on the slopes. We didn't fare much better, either.

Dad and I and the two other comedians, Marty from Canada and Rob from the UK, stayed with the chef of one of the fanciest restaurants in Meribel. Aside from the wonderful food he made us, we consumed two crates of wine in four days. One comic, who shall remain nameless, would wake up and before even getting out of bed would start drinking vodka from the glass that had been left at his bedside overnight. It was a wonderfully sinful and gluttonous trip.

One of the international tours that I had negotiated myself was to be in South Africa. I had been invited to headline an Indian Comedy Festival. I was told I could bring another comedian, so I called my friend Vidur Kapur in New York and asked him to come. Now, the way our business works is that normally the money comes in advance and then you fly out. However, my client convinced me that it would be given to me as soon as I landed, so I took the flight to Johannesburg. Prudence should have stopped me from taking that call but I had been doing comedy for less than three years and was being invited to headline an international comedy festival—so of course I took the flight. As soon as I landed, I asked for our fee and the client said he'd bring it the next day. We were then driven to a very shady looking suburb of Jo'berg and put in the pinkest flat I've ever seen. Everything was pink—curtains, bedsheets, walls, fans. It was quite a sight.

The next day, when the client came to pick us up, I asked him for our money. He said he'd give it to us later. I told him that our contract was simple and that we needed to be paid before the show. So he could go to an ATM and quickly bring us the money. He said the audience was waiting, so he wouldn't do it. I said, in that case, we weren't coming. He pulled out a revolver, stuck the barrel in my ribs and said, 'You ARE coming'. We were then driven to a mall. From the mall we were taken to an underground parking lot where a makeshift stage had been made. An audience of 500 people sat in plastic chairs. They had carried their own blankets for the show. Quite the 'festival'!

Vidur wasn't aware of the threat, so he went on and did his thing. I followed. Five hundred people in front and one man at the back with a gun in his hand. If you ask me whether I can do comedy to save my life—yes, I can.

Our last two shows in Durban were sold out. Over 1000 people were expected at each show at the Sibaya Casino and enough publicity had been done for them. We were to have had shows in Cape Town too, but those had been cancelled. At the airport, my client tried to convince Vidur to go directly to Durban with him. However, I arm-twisted him into going to Cape Town with me. We got to Cape Town and I called the organiser and said, screw you. I told him that if he didn't transfer our money immediately, we would not come to Durban and he could deal with the embarrassment in his home city. He sent some money. Enough for me to pay Vidur in full. He had come on my invitation and I felt responsible for him. Now came the conundrum. I knew the rest of the money would never come. BUT it was a 1000-seater auditorium. And it was sold out. And my logic was, surely he won't shoot me before the show. So we went. After the last show, I had a taxi waiting outside my green room door. I finished the show, got off stage and into the taxi. I went straight to the airport, bought a new ticket and took the first flight out to London.

Life threatening experiences apart, what I didn't realise was that my comedy had gone international before I had. The five-minute set that I shot for *The World Stands Up* had gone viral. A recording of the clip was put on YouTube and in those days, it got 900,000 views—before Viacom bought Paramount and it was taken down. It was probably what landed me the South Africa gigs. The last line of my set ('I come from the land of the Kama Sutra, I can fuck you in more ways than you can count.') had become wildly popular with the Indian community. People were walking up to me in almost every country I visited and asking me to repeat that line.

There was another development around this time that was more internal than external. I felt like I was slowly coming into my own. Okay, even while writing this I feel I may have gone too far with that statement, so let me just say, it was an early development. One thing was for sure. For a man who could fit in anywhere but belonged nowhere, I was finally starting to feel a sense of belonging. In an industry that largely comprised a bunch of misfits, in a strange way, I fit. I had begun to find a sense of belonging amongst others like me, who also felt like they didn't belong anywhere.

I believe that stand-up comedy is an outward expression of an inward journey. We work in a profession that has no real rules, boundaries or guidelines. Nothing is taboo. There is no social pressure with regard to what you can and cannot say. (Comics reading this and vehemently shaking their heads in disagreement, I'm talking about the UK comedy circuit in the first decade of the new millennium. This was also a time when people weren't recording your clips on their phones and posting them on the internet.) As a result, you are forced to look inward and ask yourself what you actually think about things. About what YOU find funny. What your opinion or point of view is, without being coloured by anyone or anything else. For example, I had many comics advise me not to talk about being Indian because then I would get pigeonholed in people's minds. However, as the only Indian comedian in the UK, I thought that if I didn't express the point of view of a first-generation Indian in the UK, who would? They say that it takes you ten years to 'find your voice' in comedy. To be comfortable in your own skin. That journey for me had begun.

And this then is the perfect time to recall that other transformation in my life. Ever since I first met her, I had found myself truly, madly and deeply in love with N. I wanted us to build a life together. After landing my job in London, I had encouraged her to apply to courses in the UK so she could get an international qualification and land a job there. She got admission to a teaching course in Oxford. I knew that finances were tight in her family, so I offered to pay her course fee. My family was not happy with this decision. They didn't think it was right for a twenty-four-year-old in his first job and under financial pressure to pay for his girlfriend's education. They felt that this was the responsibility of her family and they should not have allowed me to take on the burden. I felt differently. I knew that this was the girl I wanted to spend the rest of my life with and I saw it as an investment in our future. Much to my anger and disappointment at the time, my father brought the matter up with hers and the advances I had paid were eventually reimbursed to me. Now, of course, I can understand my parents' point of view, but I did not agree with it at the time.

N eventually completed her degree, landed a teaching job in London and moved to the city. I proposed to her and we got engaged. Once my sabbatical started, since I no longer needed to live close to an office, I moved out of The 171 and in September 2004 we moved into a house together. A small one-bedroom flat at 1 Durham Road in East Finchley, which was near the school where she taught. My loans paid back, us in a house together with marriage on the cards, things felt happy. And comfortable. But I wasn't prepared for what came next. It turns out that when you are in a relationship and struggling to make ends meet and build a foundation for your lives, you really stick together as a couple. You fight the odds to make things happen for yourself and the other person. But sometimes, when things get better, the relationship deteriorates. The pressure is off and you lose sight of the big picture. And that's what started happening with us.

We hadn't had an argument in eight years, yet suddenly there were things we felt we couldn't get past. Our families wanted different things when planning the wedding and we both dug our heels in. With stalemate on the cards for a while, I suggested we spend some time apart. I felt that, for a woman, a relationship needs to go somewhere, whereas we men can stay in limbo land forever. It's a broad generalisation that may not hold true, but I know it did for N. I thought that if we stayed apart for some time, either we would figure out that we were fighting over stupid things or we would figure out that it was never meant to be. As it turns out, I figured out that we were fighting over stupid things and she figured out that it was never meant to be.

I tried my best to patch up. With attempted conversations, messages via friends, and gestures both small and grand. To no avail. When she got locked out of her house on a rainy night, I scaled the outside wall of the building, climbed up to the first floor, traversed a slippery ledge, and broke in through a window so I could open the door from inside. Sure I had some rock climbing skills, but it was an incredibly risky task and only a man stupidly in love would attempt it. When she visited her aunt over the weekend, I drove over five hours to leave flowers outside her door. She still didn't see me. I can't even imagine how hard it was for her and how badly she must've been hurt to push me away like that. I remember parking my car on The Bishops Avenue, a street full of millionaires' houses, and breaking down. It was an hour before I could pull myself together and I knew as the tears rolled down my cheeks that I would never be truly happy again.

N was the love of my life. I had been with her since I was twenty. This was the woman I wanted to grow old with. I developed every single sign of clinical depression. For an entire year, I locked myself into a house (which, incidentally, was ten minutes away from hers; I had rented it in the hope that I might occasionally catch a glimpse of her). I was on a bottle of whiskey a day. It felt like my heart had broken into a million pieces and it took me years to put it back together. But somehow, even when I put it back, it didn't feel whole again. There were pieces missing. And those were pieces I didn't even want back because they would always belong to her.

In the middle of this depression, God only knows how many whiskeys down, I wrote a poem. I called it 'Pieces of my heart'.

Pieces of My Heart

The warmth of your body against mine
The smell of your hair, your skin
Your head on my chest
The way you wear your saree, the kajal in your eyes
Your beautiful, beautiful eyes

The unfinished cup of tea
The way you fall asleep on the sofa
The way you bump your head
The weak ankle, the hurting ear
Your fears, your vulnerabilities
Every little imperfection that I love you for

Your first day of college
Applying for jobs
That job offer
Shopping for your working suit
Your first pay cheque
Your first raise
I grew up with you

I still sleep on my side of the bed
Because you will be back
For it is meant to be
And one day when the sun rises and I open my eyes
You will be right there
Next to me
In your place
And I will watch you sleep again
And kiss your forehead
And hold your drowsy body in my arms
As you slumber in the sleep of my dreams.

This was the year I had started doing stand-up comedy. I don't know if it was a passion, an obsession, an escape or just a crutch. But it was the only thing that I had. Every single day, I would wake up at ten thirty in the morning and cook a meal for myself at two o' clock. I would get into some other comedian's car at around 4 p.m. We would drive to some city in the UK for a gig. We'd reach there around 8 p.m. I would be nervous, so I wouldn't eat. Frankly, if the venue didn't offer to feed me, which they often didn't for an open spot (new comic), I couldn't afford to eat out either. At the shows, sometimes there were 300 people and sometimes just three men and a dog. After the show, we'd drive back and I'd get dropped off on the outskirts of London at about two o' clock in the morning. I would pay the driver my share for the petrol. Keep in mind I wasn't getting paid for any of these shows. I couldn't afford a taxi, so I would change three different night buses to get home, sometimes waiting on the street for forty-five minutes in the cold London winter. Finally I would get home between 4 a.m. and 5 a.m. I did this every single day, for an entire year. At the end of the year, I had no money, no friends, no relationships, and no life. But every single comedy promoter in the country knew my name.

Chirag Jain was dead. And Papa CJ was born.

bringing the laughs home

In 2001, my father had a heart attack. Or rather, when he went for a medical test, he was informed that he had had one in his sleep. One of his arteries was blocked and he needed to have an angioplasty and have a stent put in. Hearing this news changed my life. I decided that I was going to try and spend as much time with my family as I could. It was a conversation with my dad that triggered the decision.

Dad did some complicated mathematics and after calculating the number of holidays I got from work and the number of days he came to visit me in the UK, he subtracted sleeping hours, washroom hours, etc. and estimated that he had hundred days left to spend with me in his lifetime. You're right in thinking this was quite a macabre conversation for a father to have with his son, nevertheless the number hit me like a slap on the face. (My editor put the word 'macabre' there. I had to Google the meaning. It means 'disturbing because concerned with or causing a fear of death.')

My father was my best friend and hero. A simple, quiet, decisive and contented man, and the polar opposite to the ball of energy and enthusiasm bouncing from one place to the other—my mother. My mother is the life of the party, always telling jokes and entertaining people while my father, when spoken to, is the storyteller who draws people in. I've spent most of my life idolising my father and like to tell myself I have inherited characteristics from both my parents, but the fact is that I am almost exactly like my mother. She and I are kites that fly in the wind and my father is the anchor we are tied to. The anchor who lets us know where home is.

Immediately after I had the hundred-days conversation with dad, I decided that I was going to move back to India as soon as I could. I didn't want to be in the UK when everyone who mattered to me was back home. So, in December 2007, I made the move.

It was interesting to move back to India as a stand-up comedian. Here was a child of middle-class parents who had attained the British equivalent of 'the American dream'. A job with a multinational company in London was definitely the epitome of the Indian middle-class dream. And this boy had returned to India to be a stand-up comedian. Ninety-nine per cent of the country didn't even know what that was.

I remember an aunty asking me, '*Beta tum kya karte ho?*' (Son, what do you do?). '*Aunty mein comedian hoon. Mein joke sunata hoon.*' (Aunty, I tell jokes. I'm a comedian.) She replied, '*Beta joke toh mein bhi sunati hoon. Tum kaam kya karte ho?*' (Son, I also tell jokes. But what do you do for a living?).

Another time, my mum was trying to explain to our domestic help what I did for a living. The only way she managed to describe it was by telling her that I was a 'joker'. Our help could not believe this was possible because jokers were four feet tall, she said. (*'Par memsahib baba joker kaise ho sakta hai? Joker toh chaar foot ka hota hai!'*). Clearly, her reference points were clowns that she had seen at the circus.

Even today, ten years after I began doing comedy in India, journalists will come for an interview and their photographers will ask me to 'make a funny face'. Or I'll be walking in a mall and someone fifty yards away will point at me and burst out laughing. They're mimicking their physical reaction when they last saw me at my job. All I can say is, I hope these people never spot porn stars in a mall!

Comedians have never been considered cool, especially in India. If I have a great gig, someone might come up to me afterwards and say 'Dude, you were a rockstar tonight'. I'm willing to bet nobody has ever walked up to a rockstar after a gig and said, 'Dude, you were a comedian tonight'. And if those words were ever said, I can guarantee they weren't received very well.

However, it was wonderful to come back home and start doing stand-up. India is a gold mine for comedy. Since I had been living abroad for eight years, I could look at my country with an outsider's eye. Oh, the things you notice. For instance, while driving in Delhi, if you want to change lanes, you never switch on the indicator. If you do that, the person who is coming from the other side will know your strategy. Unlike in the rest of the world, changing lanes in India requires stealth. Also, most people don't make enough of an effort to get out of the way of an ambulance, but should one go past, they will move planets to get just behind it to try and sail through. I wouldn't be surprised if some people have ended up going to the hospital even if it wasn't their original destination!

Another thing that hits you afresh is that in our country we still discriminate against people on the basis of the colour of their skin. We are obsessed with fair skin, and 'fairness creams' are the jewels in the crown of consumer goods companies. It's gone so far, they now have a fairness cream for vaginas. Seriously! What do people want? One that glows in the dark? What's next? Will we have a fairness cream for penises? Imagine a situation where the parents of a girl are trying to convince their daughter to marry a man in a typical arranged-marriage setup. 'We don't know his background and we don't know his salary, but his penis glows in the dark, like a lightsaber. If you marry him, the force will be with you!'

We can occasionally be quite illogical as well, and that is a great source of humour. The city of Chennai, for example, has a hospital called Aggarwal Hospital. It was built by an eye doctor, and he made the entrance to the hospital in the shape of a massive eye. Thank God he wasn't a gynaecologist!

I had hardly unpacked my bags on reaching India when, on 14 January 2008, my phone rang. It was my agent Brett. He said there was a TV show called *Last Comic Standing* in the US that wanted me to audition for them. I had never even heard of the show, let alone seen an episode. I asked him what the deal was. He said it was a free ticket to Miami. I'm a cheap date, so obviously I was on board!

Two weeks later, I was on the flight, ready for the international auditions. Three thousand people had auditioned for the show from across the United States. For my audition, I think it was about 130 comedians from twenty-seven different countries. In the morning, we auditioned for the producers. In the afternoon, for the judges. In both cases, in a nearly empty room with just two other people present. The producers and judges narrowed it down to seventeen people who would perform for the live audience that night. Some comedians had flown all the way from Australia to Miami to perform for two minutes in front of two people and to be told, that was it. Luckily for me, I had a strong set in front of the live audience and at the end of the night, I was told that I had been shortlisted for the semi-finals. Thirty-two of the 3000-odd people would be in

At the Miami Improv for the Last Comic Standing *auditions*

the semi-finals, which would be held in six weeks' time in Las Vegas. In all honesty, I still knew next to nothing about the show and its popularity. I was just excited about the fact that I'd be performing in Vegas.

Vegas, baby!

Vegas was pretty cool. We got to perform in a 2000-seater theatre at the Paris Hotel and Casino and share a green room with Las Vegas showgirls. A little over three minutes is what I was asked to do, so I fell back on what I thought were the greatest hits from my fledgling career. The show went well and I was chosen to be in the final. Twelve comedians would be thrown into a house in Los Angeles and two would be eliminated every week. I didn't have any sense of what that even meant. I remember an American comic excitedly saying that over ten million people would watch the programme. To which I jokingly replied, 'Dude, I come from India. If I open my bathroom window, ten million people will show up live!'

Being in the *Last Comic Standing* house was strange for me. Having never seen the programme or any reality TV before that, I had no context. I reserve my funny for my performances and am a regular guy off stage. Each time a camera came around in the house, some of my fellow comics would become all animated and try and be funny, whereas I just stayed normal. Also, having never performed in the US, I had no clue what bits of my material would translate for American audiences. Frankly, I'm surprised I even made it to the top ten; my best guess is they had a diversity policy!

The way the show works after you get into the house is that every week, three comics go into a head-to-head battle at a live show in Vegas and two comics are eliminated. In the second week of being in the house, I was put into a head-to-head battle against the eventual winner of the show, and was eliminated. The smart career move at that point, having a work permit in hand and a TV profile in the US, would have been to stay on in America and do stand-up there for a while. But I had just moved back to India after eight years away and I wanted to be home. So I took the flight back.

In mid-2008, I did my first multi-city tour in India. Five shows across five different cities, all of which were house full. In India, when you get paid for a show, the client deducts ten per cent tax at source, which he then pays to the government on your behalf. My promoter didn't do that because, according to him, he had made a loss in spite of

Papa laughs his way to US

OVER A CUP OF COFFEE

Less than four years into stand-up comedy, Papa CJ has become India's only finalist in America's reality television talent show – "Last Comic Standing". That puts him in the top 30 from thousands of comedians who auditioned...So saying that he has achieved a lot in a short span is understatement. From scaling an 18,000 ft peak in the Himalayas to trekking the Grand Canyon, the Oxford graduate's comedy career hasn't been a cake walk. Read further as Papa CJ shares his success story full of ups and downs, with *Shwetal Sukhija of Deccan Herald*

An Indian in the race to be 'Last Comic Standing' in US

Neelam Raaj | TNN

New Delhi: Indians have a reason to be tickled pink. A desi comedy export has made to it the finals of Last Comic Standing, a hit American show that showcases some of the world's funniest comedians. Delhi-born and Oxford-educated Papa CJ, who has just wound up his first tour of India, generated enough laughs during auditions at Las Vegas to make to it to the final list of 12 comics who will compete for the title of Last Comic Standing in the show's sixth season (back home, we're still seeing Season 2).

Papa CJ, who has performed at comedy clubs in the UK, US and South Africa, says he dumped a management consultancy job to make a career out of telling jokes. "I did it once and haven't left the stage since," he says. TV isn't a patch on live stand-up. "It is a bit like sex really — there's no substitute for actually being there."

TICKLING YOU PINK: Papa CJ

Regaling audiences with his desi brand of humour, CJ pokes fun at everything from Indian call centres (guess who was manning the phones for Big Brother) to being "randomly" selected for screening at American airports. With nothing off limits — least of all sex — this Indian comic is one of several South Asian comedians carving a niche for themselves and, in the process, propagating positive identities for the very community they kid about.

Russell Peters, of course, occupies, as he puts it, "the lofty position of being the first South Asian comic to grab that mike and hang onto it." This Canadian of Indian descent was also the first to garner multimillion dollar earnings after a pirated copy of his DVD appeared on the Internet in 2003 and spread like wildfire in a classic example of viral marketing.

Comedians Vidur Kapur, Rajiv Satyal and Vijai Nathan are other cultural hybrids who are using comedy to bridge the gap between the disparate worlds they inhabit.

"At first, people think 'who is this cocky little Indian guy' but then my jokes come from my experiences and being Indian is very much a part of that." CJ's parting joke: A Brit and an Indian face off. The Indian claims he is smarter. He proves it: 'I come from the land of Kamasutra, I can f*** you in ways that you don't even know.'

every show being sold out. That was my first introduction to business in India. 'Money talks and bullshit walks.'

In my experience, if your money doesn't come before the show, it either never comes or you'll be grovelling for it for months on end. I remember one show with a high-profile client. The show was supposed to start at 6 p.m. in Delhi. At 4 p.m., they told me, 'The signatory is travelling,' (the most common excuse by a mile) so the cheque would be given to me the following week. I told them they'd had my contract two weeks ago and without a cheque in hand I would not do the show. Miraculously, the signatory was able to fly from Mumbai to Delhi, go to the office, sign a cheque, give it to the driver, and get it to me by 5 p.m.

One of my early shows that gave me a feel for the hunger and the potential of English language stand-up comedy in India was one I did in December 2008 at the Lodhi Garden Restaurant in Delhi. We had 150 chairs set up in an outdoor space. Four hundred and fifty people showed up, most of whom stood for the duration of the ninety-minute performance. It was then that I decided I would take an active role in trying to establish and grow the comedy circuit in India.

My friend Deepali Gupta used to manage a restaurant called Mocha Bar at Nehru Place in Delhi. In early 2009, we launched open mic nights there. We called it Papa CJ's Shaken n Stirred. While we were looking to try and promote stand-up comedy, we had no clue who we would get in the room in the early days, so we opened it up to multiple genres of entertainment. On the first night itself, we had three performers who later went on to become well established names on the Indian comedy circuit, Abish Mathew being one of them.

What I wanted to ensure in those days was a supportive atmosphere for stand-ups. Standing on stage and trying to make people laugh while getting nothing from the audience in return, and then having one person say something mean to you, can be enough to crush a new comic's soul and stop

him or her from ever giving it a go again. I would therefore host the shows, try and educate the audiences on how stand-up worked, and 'manage' any unruly elements myself.

This was a wonderful time on the circuit. We had performance poets, singers, storytellers and a bunch of aspiring comedians who were extremely supportive of each other. There was a rawness, a friendliness and an earthiness to our movement, if I may call it that, which was very refreshing. Two shows stick out in my mind. One was on the night of Abish's parents' anniversary. We got them on stage, had them cut a cake, and made the entire audience sing for them before distributing cake to everyone. That was the vibe and camaraderie in that room.

The other show was when I made Raghav Mandava host for the first time. After the first half, he said it was too difficult and asked if I would take over for the rest of the show. I told him that was unacceptable and he would have to get back on the stage. Today, in my opinion, Raghav is one of the best hosts in the country. He would soon go on to run his own open mic nights under the name of Cheese Monkey Mafia in a venue called News Cafe, where he used to bartend. Many comedians you see on the Indian circuit today found their first platform in that room in New Delhi.

With other comedians starting to run their own rooms, the ball was rolling and I didn't need to organise nights on my own. Instead, I tried to support individual comedians who I thought had potential, in whatever capacity I could. This ranged from having some of them open for me at bigger gigs, giving feedback on material, joke-writing and performance skills, sometimes offering financial support

The early days of stand-up comedy in Delhi. Comedians in this photograph include Zakir Khan, Amit Tandon, Neeti Palta, Jeeveshu Ahluwalia, Nishant Tanwar, Abijit Ganguly, Vikramjit Singh, Amit Sharma, Manu Shama and Manish Tyagi.

and, on one occasion, speaking to the CEO of a company to get a young comic's job location changed so he could continue to do stand-up comedy. The company I set up organised and facilitated shows and tours for comedians in partnership with event management companies and brands. I also started a comedy course but soon found that I was putting in so much time, effort and personal attention into the work of each participant that I had little left over for myself.

Being one of the first English language stand-up comedians in the country, I started getting a lot of work. I did my second multi-city India tour in early 2009. I also wanted to expose India to world-class English language stand-up comedy. My friend Chetan had set up his own event management company at the time. We agreed to bring down some talent I knew from the UK circuit to do a four-city tour in India.

End-of-tour celebration for a twenty-gig tour organised by The Papa CJ Comedy Company. Comedians included Abish Mathew, Amit Tandon, Neeti Palta, Raghav Mandava, Appurv Gupta and Abijit Ganguly.

Paul Zerdin was a comedian and ventriloquist whom I had worked with in the UK. I had seen him destroy every room we had ever performed in together and I could think of nobody better. Paul had also performed at one of my charity fundraisers in London. His comedy was clean and accessible, and so we closed the deal. Advances were paid and the dates were locked in. This was around the time that The Comedy Store was about to open in India. They were bringing some comedians from the UK to tour under

Paul Zerdin live in Delhi. He went on to win
America's Got Talent.

their banner. They asked me to move the dates of my tour with Paul. However, both he and all our venues had been paid for and we'd have lost a chunk of money if we moved things around. Given that the sponsors who had initially committed to the tour had pulled out at the last minute, we were already losing money. However, we had made professional commitments and had to honour them. This resulted in The Comedy Store not looking upon me with any great kindness. This is something that upset me for a long time because I have great regard for Don Ward, The Comedy Store, and what they stand for. It's also a room I considered my comedy home.

Since the English language stand-up comedy circuit in India, and Delhi in particular, had taken on a life of its own, I shifted my focus to corporate events. Corporate work is some of the most lucrative work on the comedy circuit here. For an auditorium show, you have to hire a venue, get a plethora of permissions, get tickets stamped after paying entertainment tax in advance and then market the show in the hope of selling out. For a corporate gig, the money comes in advance, you show up, perform, and leave. But of course, they aren't easy gigs to play for a few different reasons. The first is the environment. Unlike music, which can run in the background, for comedy the audience needs to shut up and listen. At an auditorium show, people come with the intention to do so. However, at a corporate awards event for example, they want to have a drink and collect an award. Then the comedian is thrust upon them. That makes it a tough gig. Add to that the fact that invariably the bar is open and you are competing with food, drinks and the voices of people ordering the same.

The second challenge has to do with content. I've often joked that we are the largest democracy in the world but we are also the largest hypocrisy in the world. Every single corporate show I've done comes with the same remit: We are a respectable brand, please keep the content completely clean. However, come the day of the show, they have two drinks and tell you they want some 'masala'. They want you to do a naughty show, but in the event that a single person gets offended, they want you, the comedian, to take the bullet for it. This hurdle calls for a certain psychological gamesmanship whereby you have to get the audience to explicitly give you permission to do a show with adult content and also separate your identity from the brand you have been hired to perform for. Once that is done, you can give the people what they want.

Unfortunately, what has been happening in the corporate sector of late is that comedians who don't have the breadth of material and gravitas to hold the attention of a mature audience are being booked by event managers who want to maximise their margins. Now, comedy either works or it doesn't. There rarely is an in-between. When the inexperienced comic screws up the show or does material that may not be appropriate for the environment, the client does not say that he will not book that particular comedian again. He thinks that all stand-up comedy is like that and that he will never book any comedian again. As a result, the industry suffers.

But corporate gigs, while tough, can be really fun to do. The folks I address are not all that different from those who come to comedy clubs, they just happen to be in a different environment. An environment that's a bit formal, even stuffy. I think of them as people who have probably had a tough time at work and could really use a laugh. Once you get them on your side, it's wonderful to see them let their hair down and give in to the mood with reckless abandon.

At a corporate show in Delhi

It's the element of comedy that works best, of course, and I incorporate it in all my sessions. My 'Naked Leadership' session, for example, includes a performance from which leadership lessons are eventually drawn. In 'A Comedian's Guide to Marketing and Content Strategy' I break down how I view my business as a comedian, and then make my clients articulate their marketing strategies through that lens. The truth is, most employees are bored with the standard PowerPoint presentations and one-sided lectures. If it's not interactive and fun, you could lose them just five minutes in.

India presents some interesting and unexpected venues where I have performed stand-up. I remember doing a show for Nokia in Pune. Well, not exactly in Pune, but in Pune air space. Nokia was launching a new phone. They had painted an entire aircraft in the colours of that phone and we were to take off from Mumbai and fly over Pune in it. I would perform en route and we would land back in Mumbai. The flight was due to land in Mumbai at 3 p.m., and at 5.45 p.m., I was to catch a flight to Delhi, so I could perform at a show there at 9 p.m.

As things go in our part of the world, the performance flight took off late. They gave me a mega phone to perform. It wasn't working, so I used the PA system of the plane. In those days, you could do this without getting into trouble. Since I was on the PA, the pilots could hear me perform as well. They heckled me on the system and I heckled back. I remember making the inflight announcements and letting the passengers know how excited the captain was since this was his first flight and only the day before, he had got his licence from Nehru Place (Nehru Place at the time was known to be the destination for those seeking forged driving licences). I don't know whether it was air traffic or the pilot getting his own back at me, but our flight landed at 5.40 p.m. My flight to a sold-out show in Delhi was at 5:45. I literally ran down the stairs to the tarmac. Luckily I had my boarding card with me and I spoke to a guy on the ground, explaining my situation and the fact that I absolutely had to catch that next flight. He said, I'm sorry, but you'll have to go back to the terminal and then be escorted to the aircraft, if you can make it in time. He pointed at an aircraft about 200 yards away and mentioned that that was the plane I was supposed to catch. He then turned around to talk to someone on his walkie-talkie. Immediately, I started running towards the other plane. On the tarmac of the airport. With security running behind me. I know, had this been anywhere else in the world, a brown man running towards a plane in the post 9/11 world, I would have been shot. But I reached the aircraft, they allowed me in, shut the door, and we took off. I got to my show in Delhi fifteen minutes after the scheduled start time. I've done three shows in a night in one city, but doubling up in two different cities 2000 miles apart on the same day is something I may not want to do again!

Talking about things I may not want to do again, I was once hitching a ride back with a friend of a friend after a wedding in Delhi. They said they needed to stop over somewhere on the way and would drop me home afterwards. I agreed. I was taken to a pool party where most people were high on some drug or the other. One of the girls dived into the shallow end of the swimming pool and smashed her head. We needed volunteers to take her to the hospital, but in a matter of minutes, her 'friends' disappeared. So her boyfriend and I took her to a hospital in South Delhi. We found a doctor and her boyfriend held her legs and one arm, and I held her head and the other arm and performed stand-up comedy to distract her while the doctor put thirty-two stitches on her head.

In addition to doing straightforward stand-up comedy, I started getting invited to host events as well as work as a moderator and interviewer. A particularly tense interview became memorable for me. I was asked to interview the author Shobhaa De at an event. This was soon after the 2016 Olympics, during which she had posted a tweet that said that the goal of Team India at the Olympics was to go to Rio, take selfies and come back empty-handed. She called it a waste of money and opportunity. The tweet upset me because I felt it was deeply unfair and did not take into consideration the years of training, hard work and dedication of our athletes. I informed the organisers that I would be calling her out on this during the interview. While at first they tried to persuade me not to do so, they eventually called her and took her permission for me to ask the question. Not that I was happy to hear this, but I decided I'd go ahead and ask anyway.

Come the day of the interview, one minute before getting on stage, I was told that before the interview started, Shobhaa De would make an opening statement. I was livid. Obviously she would pre-empt all that I had planned. So I asked if I could at least invite her on to the dais. This was my welcome: 'Good morning, ladies and gentlemen. I know you are all excited about this session. Also, I know you are very keen to talk about the Olympics tweet. But let's be honest, the Olympics are far bigger than Shobhaa De and she has already addressed this subject in the past, so let's just talk about her today. Please welcome Shobhaa De.'

Shobhaa started her statement by saying, 'Thank you for the perspective that the Olympics is bigger', clearly not expecting me to interject. I did, of course, asking whether she disagreed, to which of course she said she didn't. Her opening statement was as expected, about how she used to be a sportswoman and was old enough to be the grandmother of most people in the room and therefore should be respected. As she left the dais to take her seat, I said, 'Ladies and gentlemen, the defence rests.'

I opened with the question, 'We'd like to ensure that nobody points a finger at you saying that bringing Shobhaa De here was a waste of money and opportunity and that all people did was take selfies with you. So, just to ensure that the people in this room don't feel that they leave this session *khaali haath* (empty-handed), right at the top, what do you believe an entrepreneur can learn from Shobhaa De?' The question was intended to wind her up and you could have cut the tension with a knife.

During the interview, she tried to get me to ask her about the Olympics tweet multiple times, but each time, I refrained. At the end we had an audience question-and-answer session and someone asked the question. Really, all she had to do was say she was sorry that her intentions had been misunderstood, but there was no chance in hell that she would go anywhere near anything that could be considered an apology. She eventually said that people often misinterpreted her. Which forced me to say, 'So what you're saying is that as someone who has been a professional writer for so many years, you cannot pull together 140 characters in a way that will not be misinterpreted.' That line was the straw that broke the camel's back. She said she had addressed this topic in the past and she did not want to talk about it anymore and if I asked any further questions about it, it would be a monologue. I couldn't resist reminding her that that was what I had said at the start, i.e., that she had addressed this already and we shouldn't talk about it. However, it was she who insisted we talk about it!

I must confess that such interactions were rare. I'm almost always positive and trying to get the very best out of the people I am speaking with. I remember a wonderful interaction at a two-day event I was hosting for Entrepreneurs Organisation in Calcutta in 2014. On day one, I co-hosted with Archana Vijaya (also a Calcutta girl, often seen on television anchoring the Cricket League IPL) and on the second day, she interviewed a guest while I hosted on my own. The guest she interviewed was Sushmita Sen, India's first Miss Universe.

I fell in love with Sushmita when I heard her speak. What a wonderfully intelligent, grounded and articulate woman she was. As I sat listening, she recalled an incident from her childhood when, as a little girl, she had walked into her father's room while he was watching TV with tears in his eyes. He was overwhelmed with emotion because Rakesh Sharma had just stepped ~~on to the moon~~ IN TO SPACE (he was the first Indian to do so). She asked him who the man was, to which he responded, 'I've never met him, but he is famous'. It was at that moment that she decided that she wanted to be 'famous'. She didn't know what the word meant, but she wanted to be whatever it was that it meant.

During the interview, Sushmita was asked what kind of men she liked. She said 'entrepreneurs', at which the partisan audience obviously cheered in delight. Then Archana asked her to answer the question seriously and indicate the kind of men she liked and why. She said she liked Shah Rukh Khan because he was constantly trying to improve and master new things. Then the conversation moved on to the subject of family. Sushmita's father was in the audience. She said, 'I know that my father hopes that one day, maybe not soon, I'll get married.' Eventually, it was time to wrap up the session and Archana looked at me and said, 'Papa CJ, I'm sure you have something that you'd like to say to Sushmita.'

Now, I've had moments in my life when by intention or accident I've managed to be mildly charming, but speaking for myself, what I said next knocked all such moments way back into second place. I walked up on stage and said to Sushmita, 'I just want you to know that your father told his little girl that he had never met Rakesh Sharma, but I'll be able to tell my children that I met Sushmita Sen.'

BOOM! He shoots, he scores!

She came over and gave me a hug. As she sat back down, I carried on speaking: 'And like your father, my father too hopes that one day, maybe not soon, I'll get married.'

'And I want you to know that by virtue of being a comedian, I am an entrepreneur.'

'And I'm constantly trying to improve and master new things.'

She said, 'You have exactly what it takes, bang in place, a sense of humour.'

To which I responded, 'You had me at bang in place.'

BOOM! Laughter. Applause. And I've never met her since.

With Sushmita and Archana

At the same event in 2014, the finance minister of Bengal was invited to speak. His talk ended up being political propaganda. He said that his chief minister was very humble and down to earth and still lived in a 300 sq. ft apartment. He also mentioned that she was in touch with the people as she met 2500 people in her home every morning. I couldn't help saying that if she lived in a 300 sq. ft flat and met 2500 people at home every morning, her garden must be absolutely massive. The poor man was stumped.

On the subject of being stumped, I once performed my show *Naked* in Surat, which is a small city in the Indian state of Gujarat. The show requires a table and a chair on stage and the chair they had provided was a hideous bright yellow one, with some kind of leopard print on it. So I dragged it off the stage and put it in the wings and took a plain, dark blue chair from the green room instead. Five minutes later, one of the auditorium staff came up to me and informed me that I could not use that chair. When asked why not, he pointed out that it was a 'green room chair'. I tried using simple logic and pointed out that the green room chair was for the convenience of the artist and as the artist I would find it extremely convenient if he allowed me to move the chair twenty feet away from the green room, on to the stage. I also promised that I would personally put the chair back in the green room after the show. However, the man was adamant and mentioned that another artist had disobeyed and put a green room chair on the stage and the manager of the auditorium had stopped his show midway. I was running a high fever at the time and in no state to put up an argument, let alone a fight, so I had no choice but to give in to his unreasonable demand. Before the show began, however, I told the guy. 'You mentioned that when a previous artist put a green room chair on stage, the management stopped the show. What would happen if somebody danced naked on stage?'

He said, 'I don't know, sir, nobody has ever done that before.'

I said, 'Okay, today I'll dance naked on stage and show you!' ('*Aaj mein nanga naach ke dikhaunga*'). Sure enough, during the show, I got down to my boxers and in addition to doing my best stripper moves, I went into the audience and gave an unsuspecting lady a lap dance. After the show, I walked up to the green room man and said, '*Toh kaisa laga nanga naach?*' (So, how did you like my naked dancing?) He responded, '*Sir, agar pata hota ki aap sach much mein karne waale hain toh hum aapko kursi hee de dete!* (Sir, if I knew you were actually going to do it, I would have just given you the chair!). Artist: 1; Unreasonable auditorium staff: 0.

In addition to unsuspecting auditorium staff, taking my clothes off on stage presented some other challenges as well. I have to admit that during that period, while some men did manage to briefly convince the world that a 'dad-bod' was cool, I didn't buy into the pitch and felt some social pressure to reduce the Indian man's genetic Achilles' stomach. So I joined a gym and after a year of highly irregular working out and hours of sucking my stomach in on stage, I can proudly state that at the end of fifty shows in front of over 10,000 people, a sum total of four women have complimented me on my body. Also, each time, the compliment was the same—'Nice feet'! Naturally, I did not renew my gym membership and focussed on pedicures instead.

In spite of not having a body worth ogling at, I have had my moments. In Chennai, a supposedly conservative city, while I was in just my boxers, a woman in the audience who I'm guessing was in her mid-forties, spanked my ass really hard. A few minutes later, she walked out of the auditorium. I was most upset that after having had her way with me, she didn't even have the decency to stay till the end of the show. It made me understand how some women might feel when men don't cuddle after sex. However, ten minutes after that, she returned to her seat. When I met her after the show, I asked her what happened. To which she replied, 'I was laughing so hard, my eyes were wet. And then I spanked your ass so hard, my contact lenses fell out. I had to go out to wash them and come back.'

You can spend a year in a gym making all the effort you like, pruning yourself till kingdom come, and you may get no appreciation at all. And then one day, when you're least expecting it, a woman may spank your arse so hard that her eyes fall out! My fellow men, you may as well not succumb to the beauty standards imposed on you by half-naked actors with six packs on the big screen. Just be yourself. In due course, if you're lucky, a special someone will come along and pop their eyes out just for you.

Naked performances aside, moving back to India helped me become a better comedian. I had not grown up in the UK and therefore I didn't have shared cultural references with my audience. I didn't follow their politics and I wasn't interested in their sport (mainly football). As a result, I stuck to doing jokes on stage. I was too scared to talk to the audience because I didn't have the confidence that I would be able to successfully respond to what they threw at me. Also, half the time, I struggled to understand the accent. I myself would speak slightly slower when I performed because I figured that if I was struggling to keep up with their accent, they must be struggling to keep up with mine as well. This wasn't the case in India. Coming back home allowed me to do shows where I'd spend most of the time talking to audiences and creating humour out of thin air, instead of doing jokes I had written. It raised the level of challenge for me. I had to get into a conversation and figure out a way to instantly make it funny. Of course, I did have jokes in my pocket as back up.

I also started customising a lot of material for shows. I was getting invited to perform at a variety of private events such as birthdays and weddings. At these events I'd get there in advance, speak to the host and the guests, and create material based on that. This is particularly difficult to do at weddings, where I normally host the sangeet and the age of the audience tends to range from two to ninety and sensitivities and emotions run high. However this personalisation significantly raises the level of enjoyment for my audiences because the jokes are about them and their family and friends. I started doing this customisation for internal events and corporate gigs and also at colleges. There have been times when I did up to forty-five minutes of brand-new customised content at a show, which was created from information given to me just an hour before the show. A lot of my content was also generated from college campuses and I started getting banned from many of the colleges I performed at. 'Why CJ?' I hear you ask. Well, let me tell you.

I hate it when educational institutions train students' minds to not ask questions. Forget questioning established knowledge, they don't let them question things that are blatantly ridiculous, such as some of the rules imposed on them. Particularly at engineering colleges. One college, for example, had a rule that if a boy shakes a girl's hand for longer than three seconds, it would be considered a public display of affection and there was a monetary fine for that! What!? There was another college where you could smoke if you were a foreign student, but if you were Indian you could not. How was that even legal? These things upset both the students and me, and since they were not empowered to

Performance at VIT Vellore where I ruffled a few feathers, to say the least. You can find a video of the show online.

speak up, I would go in and use humour to hold up a mirror to the college authorities. On the rare occasion, it did lead to an actual change on the ground, but more often than not, fragile egos were hurt and I got banned from the college! However, the students always loved it and other colleges would find out about what had happened and invite me to come and stand up for them.

In 2009, I was invited to perform at the Just for Laughs festival in Canada. They booked me for two shows at their festival in Toronto. One was a show that was targeted at an Indian audience and would be shot for television. The other was a TV warm up for a show called The Ethnic Show, or as I liked to call it, The Anybody Who Is Not White Show. This was at a beautiful 992-seater theatre called the Winter Garden Theatre.

Backstage with John Cleese at JFL Toronto

I had not lost my habit of hustling, so in the nine days that I spent in Toronto, I did thirteen shows. I worked a different club every night. I remember one night in particular when I felt I had grown as a comedian due to how differently I had to exercise my comedy muscles. It was the night I did three gigs in three different rooms. The first was at Yuk Yuks, a traditional comedy club. This set to an audience of 200 was like playing Jongleurs or The Comedy Store. It was just rapid-fire gags, one after the other. Next I played a room above an Irish pub, to an audience of about fifteen people. Here I just sat at the table with my audience and told stories like one would at a family dinner. A far more relaxed, easy-going and slower-paced delivery. The last of the three shows was the most interesting. It was in a room called the Vapor Lounge. I walked into the room and found about forty small tables, each of which had a bong on it. Everyone in that room was smoking marijuana. I must clarify, when I said 'bong' I did not mean that there was a Bengali at every table, just the bong that is used to smoke up. I went to the bar and asked for a whiskey. They said they couldn't give me one because they didn't have a licence to serve alcohol. Seriously? Everyone in the room was doing drugs!

Anyhow, performing there was an entirely different experience. You got on stage, cracked a joke...and then you waited! After about a minute, the punchline went through the smoke and slowly entered the brain of the first person to get the joke. And then slowly the laughter spread across the room. You had to gauge the laughter from the facial expressions as a large chunk of the audience was too stoned to actually laugh. Then you moved on to the next joke. A five-minute set at a comedy club could take half an hour in that room.

This trip was also when I met Russell Peters for the first time. He was having breakfast at the diner below my hotel and I popped in to introduce myself and say hello. To my very pleasant surprise, he knew my name. I could not have imagined it. Here was the biggest name in comedy I had ever heard of and he knew the name of a tiny Indian comedian doing stand-up comedy on a different continent. What struck me immediately about Russell was how 'normal' he was. He was a world-famous comedian who sold out stadiums across the world and had bodyguards walk with him, but he spoke to you as he might to a friend. That weekend, he invited me to hang with him backstage while he performed for around 9000 people at Dundas Square. We became friends and stayed in touch.

In 2011, Russell was hosting a special for Showtime USA. Six episodes with four comedians each would be shot and he would host all of them. It was called *Red Light Comedy: Live in Amsterdam*. On Russell and his brother Clayton's recommendation, I was invited to be a part of this special. In all honesty, as excited as I was about shooting the special, I was more excited about meeting Russell. The day he came, he invited me to chill with him in his room. His book *Call Me Russell* had just been published and he gave me a signed copy. If there was anything I took away from that afternoon, it was a desire to try and imbibe the two qualities that seemed to characterise him—humility and generosity.

As it happens, humility would be delivered to me with a swift kick in the nuts very soon. We shot the special on

a rainy Tuesday afternoon in Amsterdam, in front of an invited audience. There were maybe a hundred people there. I was the first comedian on the first show. Russell went up to warm up the audience before the show and didn't get much from them. He then welcomed me on stage. In all honesty, I struggled. I don't think I chose the right material and as hard as I tried, I could get nothing out of the first two rows. I did the best I could and hoped they would add some laughs during editing. It was only after we shot the first episode that we learnt that nobody in the first two rows spoke any English!

Most of my other international shows went better than that. I got particularly active in Southeast Asia where the comedy scene was just beginning to grow. Singapore, and then Malaysia, had a bunch of international comics coming in regularly, building up an active local community of comedians. Singapore, in particular, allowed you to do a club gig almost every night. Umar Rana's Comedy Masala had a fantastic gig on Tuesday nights, the Blue Jazz bar had a terrific open mic on Wednesdays and The Comedy Club Asia ran four gigs from Wednesday to Sunday. My favourite was their last gig at The Dutch Club, which always had a great audience.

In Amsterdam for the taping of Showtime's Red Light Comedy.
Brett is on the extreme left and this very talented group of comedians includes Hannibal Buress on the extreme right.

Singapore also had interesting one-off events. I remember performing at a beer festival where people had started drinking at four in the afternoon. I was supposed to do a forty-five-minute headlining set at 11 p.m. I had a big-built English heckler who I put down, only to hear him shout, 'I'm going to fuck you. You come outside. You come outside.' To which I responded, 'I'm sorry to disappoint, brother, but I never cum outside. I'm Indian. We did not get to a population of 1.3 billion by cumming outside.'

Singapore is also the country where I did one of my most unusual international shows. I was invited to perform at an advertising festival called Spikes at Suntec City. It felt a little bit like performing at the United Nations. There were 2000 people from all over Asia. Half of them spoke English and the other half didn't. The guys who didn't speak English had headsets and right at the back were six transparent booths with translators who would translate my jokes.

It was really interesting because I'd crack a joke and first the English speaking people would laugh. There would be a pause and then the rest of the room would laugh. When it was a really funny joke, I could see half the room laughing their heads off and the anticipation on the faces of the other half.

I had been told that the language had to be clean but the content could be anything at all. At one point, I cracked a joke that had the word 'blowjob' in it. I still remember the dumbfounded faces of the translators. They clearly didn't have a single word that could translate that word, so they had to describe the entire activity. And if you think that was funny, there was one guy on the right side of the stage doing sign language for the deaf!

Bringing the Laughs Home

My international work, beginnings of financial stability, and the recognition that came from media coverage made the experience of comedy in India quite different from the years of struggle in the UK. I'll never forget the night when I stood freezing for over an hour at a bus stop in South London at 3 a.m., soaking wet from the rain and questioning the sense of it all. In India, I was starting to achieve an element of what some people might call success. But it was all very new to me. I had no guidelines, mentors or roadmaps for how to move ahead. It was a new industry that I was keen to help establish and make a part of the new popular culture. I didn't know the 'right' way to do it. I had no artistic or entrepreneurial background. I was going on instinct and it was all trial and error.

I was once told that for people to think of you as an artist of repute, you need to have a manager. So, for about a year, I pretended to be my own manager, Ajay. In fact, sometimes I still do. Then I spoke to someone about potentially managing me. One of the things he told me was that in order to create the right perception in the market, I needed to be aloof. I could not mix freely with the audience after a show, like I was used to doing. That apparently would take away from my 'aura'. I've never understood that. And anyway, that's not me.

When I started working on the English-language comedy circuit in Delhi, a comedy scene was being born. It is no longer a scene. It is an industry. There are hundreds of comedians doing wonderful work, and not just in stand-up. Sketch, improv, storytelling…there is much talent across multiple genres. We have comedians who have gained immense popularity through YouTube, Amazon Prime and Netflix, and their talent and popularity help them fill stadiums. Some of them are good friends and there are many I've seen from the time they started. I'm thrilled for their success.

My own path is slightly different. My passion has always been live stand-up. I love looking into the eyes of my audience and seeing the smiles on their faces. I still think of stand-up comedy as a hobby. A passion. I'd go almost so far as to say it's a lifestyle choice. I didn't leave a corporate job and join a creative field to be in a rat race in the creative field. I write my own material, I perform it, I answer the phone, I close the deal, I mail the contract and I do the accounting. I still hang out with my audiences after gigs, whether they are public, private or corporate shows. There are audience members and clients who have become close friends. And I've still never refused an autograph or a photograph. The little fame or celebrity status audiences have endowed upon me are by-products of what I do and not the reason why I do what I do. As clichéd as it may sound, I've never been drawn to fame at all. It's bringing joy to people that motivates me. I'm sure I've made tons of mistakes and that there are ways of working in this industry that could lead to far greater success, in the traditional sense of the word. But I've tried not to step on other people to rise up and I've tried to lift others up whenever I can. So whether I've got it right or wrong, in the words of Frank Sinatra, I did it my way.

A public show in my home town of Calcutta

*At The Crackhouse Comedy Club in Kuala Lumpur. I've always
preferred performing in smaller venues.*

At my solo show in Stockholm, which set the
festival venue attendance record

Motivational speaking at the Sri Ram College of Commerce, Delhi

Evan Murphy

Backstage at the Kings and Queens of Comedy show at Esplanade in Singapore. Left to right: Paul Ogata, Papa CJ, Harith Iskander, Jonathan Atherton, Ronny Chieng, Kumar

On stage in front of a full house at The Sydney Opera House

Shashi Tharoor takes the stage at a Papa CJ Comedy Company event

Speaking at The India Conference by invitation of
Harvard Business School

Irrfan ✓
27 August 2016 · 🌐

Had a great time chatting with Papa CJ at #EOSpark2016 #Raipur
@EntrepreneurOrg .... He is a funny guy 😊

···

Audience interaction after I interviewed actor Irrfan Khan

Receiving the Best Stand-up Comedian in Asia Award in Malaysia

till death do us part

Thanks to the corporate shows I was doing, I had finally started making what one could call a half-decent living. In India, once you reach a certain age and start doing reasonably well on the career front, society starts to put pressure on you to find a life partner and get married. In fact, asking young people when they will 'settle down' is a pastime as old as our civilisation itself. Basically, finish school, college, a postgrad degree, get a job, get married, have two babies, and then you are 'settled'. That's the broad gist of it. And the kind of advice you are given is also ridiculous. One of the most common is this—If you are looking to marry a girl, first look at her mother because in twenty years' time, she will be like her mother. Someone actually added to that statement and told me, '*Haathi ka bachcha haathi hee hota hai. Kuch aur janwar toh nahi ho sakta.*' (An elephant's child has to be an elephant. It can't possibly be another animal.) How, oh how, can anyone argue with such irrefutable logic? So now I'm supposed to go around town looking for what—elephants? Mothers of twenty-somethings? Walk up to a girl at a bar and say, 'Hey, I couldn't help noticing you are sitting on your own. Can I buy your mom a drink?'

Eventually I met a girl and we got married. I don't have much to say about marriage, however, because a year and a half later, I filed for divorce. The road leading to our divorce was not an amicable one and while I'm sure it wasn't easy for my ex-wife either, the physical, mental and emotional stress that I suffered on account of it made those years some of the hardest of my life.

Coping with a divorce, whether it is your decision, your partner's or a mutual one, isn't easy at all. When you get married, it feels like your life is on a train track. You think you know the general direction you're going in, with the odd deviation every now and then. But when you get divorced, it's like somebody just picked you up and dropped you in the middle of an open desert and said, 'Off you go'. It's the loneliest feeling ever.

We may be in the twenty-first century, but in India there's still a huge social stigma over divorce. What people don't realise is that a divorce can happen to anyone. Because over time, in every kind of relationship, things can change. Even small things, like what you call your partner. First it's her name, then a nickname, then 'baby', then 'my love', then 'the defendant'.

Yet, once you get divorced, people treat you differently. Once, a fellow came up to me and the conversation went something like this.

He: CJ, you are divorced. You must be depressed. You should turn to religion, to Jesus. Jesus was great. He came back from the dead.

Me: Listen, I am Hindu. We come back again and again and again and again...so that doesn't really impress me much.

He: Yes, but you know, Jesus suffered. He knows about suffering.

Me: Listen, according to Hinduism, when we get married, we are married to the same person for seven lifetimes. Don't talk to me about suffering, all right?

The other strange thing that happens after a divorce is that people start coming to you to ask for advice. Relationship advice! It's like going to a South African and asking him to teach you how to win the cricket World Cup. It's like asking Arnab Goswami to show you how to whisper on a TV debate. We have no clue!

But the worst part about being a divorcee is that you became an example to your family. A cautionary tale. I already hear my aunts saying to younger nephews and nieces, 'You should get married early. Look at CJ. He got married at the age of thirty-three and look at his life now. He is alone. He has no responsibilities. He wakes up whenever he wants, travels the world, and sleeps with whoever he likes…Do you want to end up like that?'

a knock on the door

My divorce handed me a far greater loss than I was prepared for. I have a baby boy. His name is Ishaan Jain. He was born on 30 January 2012. I have seen him once in the last seven years. I last saw him in the Mediation Centre of the Supreme Court of India. He was nineteen months old then.

The time I saw Ishaan before that, he was six months old. It was the morning of 3 August 2012. The morning that I knew my marriage was over. Also a morning when I knew that given his tender age at the time, he would need to remain with his mother. The twenty minutes during which she went for a shower will forever be etched in my memory.

If I close my eyes, I am immediately transported to the bedroom with little Ishaan lying on the bed. The whole world fell away, he was the only person who existed. His touch, his smell, the way he cooed and gurgled, his laugh…I didn't know when I would be able to see him again and I wanted to capture everything about him and that moment in a box and keep it in my heart forever. I was trying to put every ounce of my soul into every second I had with him. I wanted those moments to soak into every fibre of my being. I hugged him and kissed him and told him that I loved him.

I apologised for not being able to remain with him. And I prayed that I would get a chance to see him and hold him again, soon.

Sadly, it was thirteen months before I got to see him again. 5 September 2013. The Supreme Court of India had instructed that my son be brought for the mediation proceedings. I still remember the day I was going to see him in court. I can't tell you how scared I was. He was a nineteen-month-old baby boy who hadn't seen his father in thirteen months. The fear that my own child would not recognise me. The fear that he would push me away. The fear that I would say, 'I love you, beta,' and he would shun me. That fear of rejection. I can't even begin to describe how it felt.

As it happened, Ishaan warmed to me instantly and we spent twenty minutes laughing and playing with the toys that I had carried for him. Yet, that was the last time I saw him.

I am privileged to have shared a beautiful relationship with my own father. He was, and still is, my best friend. He has been with me through thick and thin and not just emotionally. At the age of sixty-five, he physically accompanied me to every divorce hearing. Along with mom, he has been there for every new show I've tried out. He has been present at every doctor's appointment and when I land at the airport, day or night, he is there to pick me up. The joy and strength I have drawn from the relationship I share with my parents is immeasurable. Nothing gives me more courage than having my dad put his arm around me saying, 'Go for it, son. I've got your back.' A relationship like that is what I wanted for my son as well. However, I don't get to see him and he doesn't get to see me. Knowing that you have a child who is alive on this planet and not being able to see him is something I wouldn't wish on my worst enemy.

While initially I had filed for interim custody of Ishaan, I eventually decided not to pursue the fight. I've seen far too many cases where custody battles have gone on for years and I did not think it was fair for a child to have to meet his father in a court and to only see his parents being acrimonious with each other. I thought it was better for him to grow up under one roof with one set of values and to meet whenever his mother or he wanted to. Better for him and maybe for me. Just maybe.

They say that when you become a parent, you become a softer, kinder human being. I don't know when I'll see Ishaan next. It could be ten years, fifteen years or more. I don't know what he will hear about me from the world. But on the off chance that what he hears is negative, my motivation to prove that wrong will push me to be the best human being that I can ever be.

The fact is that I am built to try and find the positive in every situation. I did get to spend some time with my son. I got to name him. Naming a child is very special and as anyone who has named a child will tell you, you learn valuable life lessons from it. The most important lesson you learn is that you should never ask your friends for advice. Because your friends are bastards. I remember telling a friend, 'If I have a daughter, I think I'll call her Priyanka'. Her response—'I had a friend called Priyanka. She was a slut.' What! But I understand, because I can be a bastard as well. A friend of mine, Rohit Kaul, had a son. He called me to ask for suggestions for names. I said, 'I think you should call him Booty. Imagine him giving attendance in class. Booty Kaul? Yes ma'am!'

When my closest friend Chetan and his wife were having their first baby, they were at the Fortis Hospital in Delhi. He was up on the second floor, where all the operation theatres were, and the rest of us were waiting downstairs. About five minutes after the operation had begun, he called me on the phone and said, 'CJ, I'm damn nervous, please come up and wait with me.' I said, 'Sure' and walked up. When I got to the door of the second floor, a female security guard stopped me and said, 'Sorry sir, *upar sirf ek aadmi allowed hai.*' (Sorry sir, only one man is allowed upstairs). I replied in a heartbeat, *'Dekhiye. humein pata nahi ki bachche ka baap kaun hai. Toh jab tak bachcha nahi niklega hum dono toh khade hee rahenge.'* (You see, we don't know who the father is. So until the child comes out, both of us have to stand and wait.) The poor woman was so flabbergasted, she just said, *'Haan haan sir, aap please jao.'* (Yes, yes sir, you please go.)

After little Nainika was born and was wheeled out of the operation theatre, the guard sneaked up to me and whispered in my ear, 'Sir, did you figure out who the father is?' I replied, 'It's neither of us.' It was years before I told Chetan's wife this story and she understood why the hospital staff gave her such dirty looks when she got out of the operation theatre.

In summary, my friends, have I had the best life ever? Maybe not. Have I had the worst life ever? Most definitely not. I am a positive guy. I do believe the glass is half full.

I do believe that I will find love. I respect independent women…and prenuptial agreements. Do I think my life will be without problems going forward? Of course not. I'm a comedian. By the very nature of what I do, I have problems that nobody else does. I'll go to a party and someone will say, 'Oh, you're a comedian, tell me a joke.' It's very irritating. What's even worse is that people come to you and want to tell you jokes. It's normally drunk men above the age of sixty, who will tell you a joke that goes on for fifiteen minutes and has no punchline. They'll end by saying, 'You can use this in your shows'. That being said, the other day a gorgeous girl came up to me and said, 'Papa CJ, people tell me I'm quite witty. I must try my wit out on you sometime.' To which I replied, 'Well, people tell me I'm quite cocky…'

At the end of the day, the fact remains that making people laugh is the only way I know how to process my pain. In spite of all the jokes I've cracked, I cannot deny that in the deepest recesses of my heart, I hope that one day, someday, there's a knock on my door. And a young man will walk in. And he will say, 'I'm looking for Papa CJ'. And as I always do, I will say, 'My name is Papa CJ, but you can call me CJ, everyone calls me CJ.' And he will say, 'Well, actually, my name is Ishaan Jain. And if it's all right by you, I'd prefer to call you Papa.'

epilogue

the papa cj happiness project

Growing up in the kind of middle class family I did, I've never liked the word 'celebrity'. That word always conjured up an image of inauthentic people at Page 3 parties air kissing each other and then bitching about the person they just met seconds after they were out of earshot. After having gained a little bit of popularity for my profession, occasionally people started referring to me as a celebrity (albeit a Z list one). This made me extremely uncomfortable until the time I could come up with a definition of the word that I could live with. That definition is this: 'Celebrity is a currency and what matters is how you choose to spend it'.

I'd like to spend the little currency that I have making a qualitative difference to the lives of others. Over the years I've learned that uplifting people is what gives me joy. That manifests itself in multiple ways.

The first of course is making people laugh through my comedy. I also work as a coach and motivational speaker at corporate organisations and universities. This allows me to equip others with the skills and attitudes to realise their dreams. However, what gives the most meaning to my work is my Happiness Project.

When I first started doing comedy, a fellow Oxford alumnus and I set up a charity to support underprivileged children in India. Even as a new act who wasn't getting paid for his shows, I would encourage my audiences to donate towards the charity if they liked my work. Once a year, at The Comedy Store in London, I'd organise a fundraiser for our charity. I was honoured that some of the best comedians in the UK, most of whom I had worked with on the circuit, donated their time and talent to perform at these shows.

At some point I started doing stand-up comedy and laughter yoga in hospitals. I did this for doctors, nurses, patients and their carers. When I travelled abroad in particular, I wanted to ensure that as an Indian comedian I brought a little bit more goodwill on behalf of my country than that which came from commercial shows. More often than not, people who are seeing you for the first time don't remember your name, but they remember you as 'that Indian

I can't find the second poster, but the line up for Great Comedy for a Great Cause 2 included Alistair Barrie, Tony Hendriks, Paul Zerdin, Scott Capurro, Paul Sinha, Sean Meo, Stephen K Amos, Jarred Christmas and John Ryan. Anyone familiar with the UK circuit will validate that the comedians who donated their time for each of these three shows are giants in their domain. I'm extremely grateful to each of them.

comedian'. ('Comedian brings laughter to hospitals'
video on YouTube)

The official birth of 'The Papa CJ Happiness Project'
took place in 2017. I had lost a big client contract
and, to my own surprise, the loss of income didn't
bother me at all. Then I thought to myself, why not do
shows for people for whom that money would mean
a lot. So I put out an open offer to charities that for
a limited period of time I would do free fundraiser
shows. The deal was that the charity would get fifty
per cent of the funds raised and the balance fifty per
cent would be given to a charity of my choice. I did
this because many of the charities that wrote in to me
did not have the bandwidth or resources to organise a

large show. However, they were doing wonderful work on the ground. I would get them to partner with a larger charity, support them in marketing, and share in the proceeds. I ended up doing seven shows across six cities in India and within a span of two weeks we raised over US$60,000 for ten different charities. They included charities that worked with underprivileged children, women and animals, as well as some that focussed on building educational infrastructure. ('The Papa CJ Happiness Project' video on YouTube)

In 2018 I put out an open offer to visit people who had been suffering from long-term or serious illnesses in their homes and hospital rooms and bring cheer to

Laughing with patients at the Max Institute for Cancer Care

them and their families for just a little while. This is probably the most gratifying work I've done in my life. I performed in a hospital room for two people and in a hospital waiting room for over two hundred. I went to people's homes and performed in their living rooms and bedrooms. I taught them laughter yoga so they could make laughter a daily occurrence even after I was gone. I saw family members cry tears of joy because they hadn't seen their loved one laugh like that for years. I've had cancer patients tell me that they haven't laughed so hard since they were first diagnosed with the disease. (See 'Fighting Cancer with Laughter' video on YouTube)

I don't know what shape or form my Happiness Project will take going forward and I'm well aware that I'm no saint. However I will do whatever I can within my own capacity to bring joy to the lives of those I come in contact with. After a performance in the bedroom of an eighty-year-old lady who'd had her leg amputated, I told her that I had lied about the performance being for free. I told her that as 'payment' I expected to receive a laughing photograph of hers every day. Three days later her son sent me a message saying I had increased her life span. He wrote that now, before he sends me his mother's photograph, she wants to look at it to make sure she is looking nice. I can't possibly ask for more.

Piyush Chopra @piuchopra · 14 May 2018

Thank you @PapaCJ for bringing so much happiness home on #MothersDay! Mom was in the ICU for 4 months, we have a lot of laughter to catch up on - thanks for the headstart! #HappinessProject2018

Nitin Batra
@batranitin

Follow

Thank you @PapaCJ for making the evening soooo special for mom & for all of us. Guys here's a noble soul among us.... He's definitely increased her lifespan this evening. Papa CJ rocks....

10:53 PM - 2 May 2018

acknowledgements

Stephen King said, 'To write is human. To edit is divine.'
I must thank my editor, the divine Karthika V.K., for her
patience more than anything else. I'm a reluctant writer and
I knew that once I committed to writing the book, I would
have to do it. So I signed the contract two years after it was
offered to me and even after that I took my own sweet time.
That was until she kindly offered to give me a swift kick in
the rear end.

A first book is special, and many thanks are due to
Gautam Padmanabhan for taking a gamble on me. There
aren't many publishers who would take a chance on a first-
time author without having read a single page of his or her
writing. Let's hope this doesn't come back to bite you in
the bum, GP!

While it isn't standard protocol to thank competing
publishers, I'd also like to thank Ananth Padmanabhan and
Diya Kar at HarperCollins for making the time to discuss
and explore the idea of this book with me. Chiki Sarkar at
Juggernaut was gracious enough to counsel me along my
writing journey.

Adil Bhatia has helped me with creative stuff for as long
as I can remember, and this book was no exception. Thank

you for designing the cover, buddy. Steve Best, I love your work and the photo on the front cover has been my pick right from the start. Thank you for it. Tarunima Sen had to suffer the trauma of shooting someone whose only response to a camera in front of him is to smile. Sorry, and thank you for the photograph on the back cover. Thanks, too, to Vishwajyoti Ghosh, Sonakshi Sinha and Rajinder Ganju, for their able support in designing the book.

Amrita helped me think about the layers that go into a book and dig a little deeper. To the many other friends who read my drafts and gave me constructive feedback, thank you. Shreya, in particular, went through many rounds of this. My buddy and ex-boss Nick Coleman gave me extensive and valuable feedback. Reeva and Aishwarya, thank you too. Debu and Divya, I love you.

Chetan, as I wrote this book I realised that apart from my parents, you have been the only constant through my life. You are a guiding light and I am truly blessed to have you as a friend. None of my life's endeavours are undertaken without your counsel, nor this book.

I would not be here today if it wasn't for the support and encouragement I received when I was starting out on my comedy journey. I'm incredibly grateful to all the promoters who gave me work, to all the comedians who took the time to give me advice, and to my wonderful manager and agent in London, Brett, who took me under his wing very early on. To The Comedy Store (Don, Charlotte, Alex, the two Simons, Loki, Kim, and literally everybody there), you are and will always be my spiritual comedy home and my favourite club in the whole wide world. To Jongleurs (Maria,

Rosie, Donna) and Mirth Control (Geoff and Jane), both my learning and bank balance would be far less if it weren't for your gigs.

To all those who supported me in my journey on the UK circuit—the lovely Julia Chamberlain, Off the Kerb and Avalon for some of those early gigs, Peter at Downstairs at the Kings Head and Ian Wilson for giving me my first television break on *The World Stands Up*. Karen, Ed, Charlie and the wonderful Alex Petty—thank you for your support in Edinburgh. All of you helped me lay the foundation that my comedy career has been built on. Susan and Jorge for inviting me to Australia.

This book is based on my show *Naked*. Roshan Abbas, you were instrumental in helping me think about the show, and Judy Balan, your input was much appreciated. I thank you.

~

I write this book with an immense sense of gratitude. For I have lived a truly wonderful life.

I grew up in Calcutta, which to my mind is one of the nicest cities in the world for a child to grow up in. The warmth and simplicity of the people makes for a great childhood. And it gives you a sense of grounding that is difficult to shake off. I know no other city that has a heart like Calcutta does. No matter where in the world I travel or stay, Calcutta will always be the place that I call home.

I spent nine years in a boarding school in the mountains breathing fresh air, drinking clean water and living countless interesting and fun experiences. I played sport for my school, went on an exchange programme, acted in plays, was school captain, learnt to play a musical instrument, learnt carpentry, clay modelling, and even tried my hands (and feet) at kathak! I have formed great friendships. Some of these friends still bring great joy to my life and there are some whom I am grateful to but have not seen in the last twenty years!

I have spent many years struggling to stand on my own feet and become financially independent. I've known what it is like to not walk into a coffee shop in the UK for an entire year because I couldn't afford a cup of coffee in there. I've known what it is to wait for a bus at 3 a.m. in the morning for over an hour in sub-zero temperatures because I didn't have the money to pay for a taxi. I've known what it is like to eat one meal and travel eight hours every day for an entire year, at the start of my comedy career. As with all struggles, I have placed great value on these experiences after having been through them and not while actually living them. On the flip side, I've rubbed shoulders with some of the richest and most privileged people on the planet and spent nights in hotels that I could never dream of affording myself. I'd like to think I haven't let these experiences go to my head.

I have had the privilege, and yes, it is a privilege, of making thousands of people laugh. Of seeing them throw away every care in the world, even if for only a little while, and just be happy.

I have performed on a plane, in a bus, on a boat, on a train, at comedy clubs, theatres, universities, hospitals, palaces, and even at a police station! I have performed at comedy shows, corporate shows, weddings, birthdays, anniversaries and baby showers. I haven't done a *suhaag raat* (wedding night) yet, but you never know, that day might come!

My audiences have ranged from the age of two to ninety. I've had a gun pointed at me before a show and knives pointed at me after a show. I've worked with some lovely and extremely funny people in many countries all over the world and I have not only learned a lot from them, but have also had the privilege of sharing a stage and a nightcap with them.

I have had an eighty-six-year-old woman walk up to me and say, 'Thank you so much, beta, I haven't laughed so much in thirty years'. And on countless occasions in India and abroad, I've had people come up to me after shows and tell me that I make them feel proud to be Indian. These kindnesses have given great meaning to my work.

Having surpassed the twenty-first anniversary of my twenty-first birthday, I have known what it is like to consider chopping off one grey hair from my left sideburn (which, incidentally, I haven't done...yet). I have also known what it is like to have to loosen my belt buckle by one notch when I sit down for a meal (which, incidentally, I have done many, many times).

I have friends who are like brothers, and friends who are like sisters, and friends who would have been like sisters had certain other wonderful experiences not been shared with them. I have friends who stick by me through thick and thin and who share their lives and the lives of their adorable children with me. Whether or not they would give their lives for me, there are those whom I would give my life for. And that means more to me because it shows how they have made me feel about our friendship and the place they hold in my heart.

I have an extended family that is full of wonderful, wonderful people. People who I love not just because I am related to them but also because they are fantastic human beings with hearts that are larger than the size of recent scams in India. I have a family that is full of 'rocks'—rocks that stand by you in hard times and rocks that go in your drink in good times. Aunts, uncles, brothers, sisters…the love and strength I get from them is invaluable. I was privileged to have two grandmothers whose emotional wisdom I can only hope to possess one day.

I have parents who, if we Hindus are right about rebirth, I pray will be my parents in every lifetime. There isn't a single moment in my entire life when they put themselves before me—from the larger things in life to putting the best piece of chicken on my plate. As a family, we didn't have much material wealth while I was growing up, but not once, not once, did I feel that I lacked anything. Ever. And they gave me the greatest gift ever: their time. They do that even now, and I continue to value that gift every day.

I have truly led a wonderful life that I can only be grateful for. I was born on International Women's Day and in the course of my life I've had the privilege of meeting, spending time and sharing experiences with some amazing women. Their compassion, strength and ability to hold it all together while overcoming great challenges has been inspirational.

Acknowledgements

I have known what it is like to love selflessly with all my heart until there is nothing left to give. I have known what it is like to be loved in the same way. I have also known what it is like to lose that love. I am not sad for it, but grateful to have had a few years when I could feel the way I felt then. For it taught me what great strength can be drawn from love. It taught me the vastness and potential of the heart to keep loving and giving even when you think the tank is empty. Not a car has been made that has the fuel efficiency of the heart! It can not only give without receiving, but can also get great joy and fulfilment from it.

To all the people who have been in my life in any capacity at all, I thank you. Your presence has shaped my life and enriched it. For that reason, while I guarantee you will get no share of the royalties from this book, I thank you.

God bless!